HACKED BY HISTORY

Seven Secrets of Dominating the Age of AI

DISHANT KHARBANDA

Clever Fox® PUBLISHING
Chennai • Bangalore

CLEVER FOX PUBLISHING
Chennai, India

Published by CLEVER FOX PUBLISHING 2026

Paperback ISBN: 978-93-7500-353-3
Hardbound ISBN: 978-93-7500-807-1

CONTENTS

PROLOGUE

Why History, Why Now

This book began during a pandemic, which is another way of saying it began during a moment when the world stopped pretending it knew what was coming next.

In 2020, while the planet locked itself indoors and watched its certainties dissolve — about work, about normalcy, about the systems we had assumed were permanent — I found myself thinking not about the virus, but about the pattern. About the fact that this was not the first time humanity had faced a shock it could not have predicted and was not prepared for. It was not the hundredth time, or the thousandth. It was simply the latest in an unbroken chain of disruptions stretching back to the beginning of the species. Plagues, wars, revolutions, collapses — the details change, the dynamic does not. Something arrives that the existing order cannot absorb. The order breaks. And the people who survive, the people who build what comes next, are not the ones who saw it coming. They are the ones who carried, inside themselves, capacities that held their value no matter what the world threw at them.

I had been thinking about artificial intelligence for years before the pandemic. In 2017, when Google published the research paper that introduced transformer architecture — the technical foundation for everything that would follow, from language models to generative AI — I stood on a stage and told an audience of educators that this technology would reshape every sector of their lives within a decade. Some nodded politely. Most were sceptical. It was 2017. AI was still an abstraction for most people. The future felt distant, and the present felt stable.

The pandemic ended that feeling of stability for everyone. And it gave me something I had not had before: time. Time to sit with the questions that had been accumulating for years. Not technical questions — what can AI do, how fast is it evolving, which jobs will it replace. Those questions have a thousand analysts working on them, and the answers change monthly. The questions that held me were older and, I believed, more important. What does it mean to be human when machines can think? What capacities matter when your expertise can be replicated in seconds? What has always survived — not just one disruption, but every disruption, across every civilisation, in every era?

I went looking for answers in the last place most people look: the past.

What I found were seven stories. Seven individuals — separated by thousands of years, thousands of miles, and completely different civilisations — who each arrived at a lesson so fundamental that it held its value across every subsequent upheaval in human history. A philosopher in Athens who was killed for asking questions. A swordsman in Japan who won sixty-one duels through the quality of his attention. A terrified astronomer in Poland who hid the truth for three decades. A psychiatrist who found meaning inside a death camp. A poet who may never have existed. An old man who wrote five thousand characters and disappeared. A nomad who built the largest empire in history on a foundation of trust.

None of them knew about the others. None of them could have imagined the age you are living in. And yet every one of them speaks directly to the crisis — and the opportunity — of this moment. Because the crisis is not artificial intelligence. The crisis is the question that artificial intelligence forces you to confront: if the machine can do what you do, then who are you?

This book is my answer. Or rather, it is the beginning of an answer, assembled from the only source I trust more than any algorithm: the accumulated experience of human beings who faced impossible situations and found, inside themselves, something that could not be taken, could not be replicated, and could not be made obsolete.

A word about how to read this book. It is structured in three acts — Awaken, Become, Endure — containing seven stories, each told across three chapters. The first chapter of each story is the narrative: the history, told as vividly and honestly as I could manage. The second chapter is the lesson: what the story teaches, and why it matters more now than in any previous era. The third chapter is the future: not predictions, but possibilities, divided into what could go right and what could go wrong, with the lesson holding true in both directions.

You can read the stories in order — they are designed to build on each other, with each one handing a question to the next. Or you can begin with whichever story calls to you. The book will hold either way.

But I will ask one thing of you before you begin. Put aside, for the duration of these pages, the assumption that the future belongs to technology. It does not. Technology is a tool. It has always been a tool. The future belongs to the human being who picks it up — and the quality of the mind, the character, and the courage they bring to the act.

Seven people across three thousand years proved this. Their stories are waiting. The eighth story — yours — has already begun.

ACKNOWLEDGEMENTS

A book about seven individuals who changed the world might give the impression that important things are accomplished alone. Nothing could be further from the truth. This book exists because of people who believed in it, argued with it, and refused to let me settle for anything less than what it could be. So my thanks and regards:

To Mr R.M. Hasnani who contributed with his unconditional support and his visionary insights into the future of artificial intelligence. Long before this book had a shape, you saw what it could become. Your conviction carried me through the periods when mine wavered, and your intuitiveness of where technology is heading sharpened every argument in these pages. This book is immeasurably better for your presence in its journey.

To Professor David Faulkner, Emeritus Professor and former Director of the MBA at the Saïd Business School, University of Oxford — for his mentorship, his guidance, and his extraordinary patience in holding through the kind of profound academic debates that most people would have walked away from long ago. Working alongside you as Deputy Programme Architect of the Socratic Fellowship has been one of the defining privileges of my professional life. Your intellectual rigour and your belief that education must be transformational, not transactional, runs through every chapter of this book, whether you see it there or not.

To Yuval Noah Harari, whose writing showed me what a history book could be when it refuses to stay in the past. Sapiens and Homo Deus gave me permission to believe that a book about history could be, at its core, a book about the future. If these pages carry even a fraction of the ambition your work embodies, I will consider the effort worthwhile.

To Yuliya Kozachenko my sounding board, and the wall I could hit with any random thought. You absorbed the half-formed ideas, the contradictions, and the scary and beautiful stories around machine intelligence. You always returned them with clarity, honesty, and the kind of unsparing feedback that only someone who genuinely cares about the work can give. Every writer needs a person who tells them the truth.

To my friends and family — for the support, the belief, and the patience that a project of this scope demands from everyone in its orbit. You endured the absences, the distraction, the dinner conversations that veered inexplicably into sixth-century China or thirteenth-century Mongolia. You did not always understand what I was doing, but you never stopped believing I should do it. That is a gift more valuable than any of you know.

To my father, Ramesh Kharbanda, to whom this book is dedicated. The lessons in these pages — about questioning, about integrity, about the courage to hold onto what matters when the cost is real — are lessons I learned from you before I found them in any history book. Your wisdom, your resilience, and your love continue to guide me beyond your presence.

And to every student, educator, and thinker who has sat across from me at a conference, in a classroom, or over a cup of tea and challenged me to think more clearly, more honestly, and more bravely about what the future demands of us.

To the mothers and every woman who nurtured me and the seven characters in this story, shaping who they would become and how they would change the world forever.

"This book is a submission of my story, your story,
our story — of the future. I hope it earns the conversation."

ACT I

AWAKEN

How to Think

1. Socrates:

The Father of Western Philosophy
Statue of Socrates in front of the Academy of Athens

CHAPTER 1.1

THE MAN WHO KNEW NOTHING

In the spring of 399 BCE, Athens was the most extraordinary place on Earth. A city of perhaps two hundred and fifty thousand people, perched on a rocky peninsula in the Aegean, had somehow produced more ideas in two centuries than most civilisations produce in two millennia. Democracy had been invented here. Theatre was performed here. The foundations of Western philosophy, mathematics, medicine, and history were being laid, in real time, by people who walked the same dusty streets, argued in the same open markets, and drank the same rough wine.

Athens was also a city on edge. It had recently lost a devastating war to Sparta — a humiliation that had shattered its confidence and left its politics volatile, its citizens suspicious, and its leaders desperate for someone to blame. A brutal oligarchy had briefly seized power, executed hundreds, and been overthrown in turn. The restored democracy was fragile, nervous, and looking for threats.

It was in this atmosphere — brilliant and paranoid, creative and dangerous — that a seventy-year-old stonemason's son was put on trial for his life. The charge was deliberately vague: corrupting the youth, and failing to honour the gods of the city. The real offence was simpler and far more dangerous. For decades, this man had been walking up to the most powerful, most confident, most respected people in Athens — generals, politicians, poets, craftsmen — and asking them questions.

His name was Socrates. And the questions were devastating.

He did not look the part. Every account agrees on this. Socrates was ugly — strikingly so, even by the forgiving standards of the ancient world. He had a flat, broad nose, bulging eyes, thick lips, and a belly that suggested no particular interest in physical discipline. He walked barefoot through Athens in the same worn cloak regardless of the season. He had no wealth. He held no office. He wrote nothing — not a single word, in an age that revered the written text. He had no school, no students in the formal sense, no curriculum. He simply talked to people.

But the talking was unlike anything Athens had encountered. Socrates did not lecture. He did not proclaim. He did not stand on a platform and deliver truths. He asked questions. Simple, polite, almost innocent-sounding questions. And the questions had a way of unravelling everything.

He would approach a general — a man celebrated for his bravery in battle — and ask: what is courage? Not what courageous deeds have you done. Not what does courage look like. What is it? Define it. The general, confident at first, would offer a definition. Courage is standing firm in battle. Socrates would nod, consider this, and then ask: is a man who stands firm out of ignorance — because he does not understand the danger — courageous? The general would pause. No, that is foolishness. So courage requires knowledge of the danger? Yes. Then is courage a kind of wisdom? The general would shift uncomfortably. Perhaps. Then could a person show courage outside of battle — in facing illness, in telling a difficult truth, in enduring poverty with dignity? The conversation would continue, and with each question, the general's original definition would crack a little wider, until what had seemed solid and obvious at the start lay in pieces on the ground, and the general — the expert, the authority — was forced to admit that he did not actually know what courage was.

Socrates did this to everyone. Politicians who claimed to understand justice. Poets who claimed to understand beauty. Craftsmen who claimed to understand excellence. He did not do it with malice. He did not mock or humiliate, at least not intentionally. He appeared to be genuinely curious — a man who believed, or claimed to believe, that he himself knew nothing, and was simply trying to find someone who knew something. The problem was that he never found one.

The Oracle at Delphi, the most sacred prophetic voice in Greece, had reportedly declared Socrates the wisest man alive. Socrates claimed to be baffled by this. He set out to disprove it by finding someone wiser. He questioned everyone he could find. And each time, the result was the same: the people who were most certain of their knowledge turned out, under examination, to not possess it. The poet could not explain what made a poem beautiful. The politician could not define the justice he claimed to uphold. The general could not articulate the virtue he was celebrated for.

Socrates concluded, with what must have been either genuine humility or exquisite irony, that the Oracle was right — but only in this narrow sense: he was the wisest man in Athens because he was the only one who knew that he did not know. Everyone else carried the additional burden of believing they understood things they did not.

For a while, this was tolerable. Athens valued argument. It valued intellectual combat. The Agora — the open marketplace at the heart of the city — was not just a place to buy olives and cloth. It was where ideas were tested in public, where reputations were made and destroyed through the quality of one's reasoning. Socrates was an irritant, but he was also, in a sense, the purest expression of what Athens claimed to admire.

But admiration has limits, and Socrates had a gift for finding them. His questions did not merely expose ignorance. They exposed the gap between what people claimed to be and what they actually were. A politician who could not define justice was not just intellectually embarrassed. He was publicly revealed as someone who wielded power over others without understanding the principles that were supposed to govern its use. A general who could not define courage was exposed as a man who sent soldiers to die in the name of a concept he could not explain. The questions were not academic. They were, in the deepest sense, political. They threatened the legitimacy of the people who ran the city.

And so Athens, the city that had invented free inquiry, decided to put its greatest questioner on trial.

The trial took place in the People's Court, before a jury of five hundred citizens drawn by lot. The prosecution argued that Socrates corrupted the young and introduced strange new gods. The real accusation, everyone understood, was broader: this man has spent thirty years making the powerful look foolish, and we have had enough.

Socrates's defence, as recorded by his student Plato, is one of the most remarkable documents in human history. He did not beg. He did not flatter the jury. He did not promise to stop. Instead, he did exactly what he had always done: he asked questions. He questioned the motives of his accusers. He questioned the logic of the charges. He questioned what Athens would become if it executed a man for the crime of thinking out loud.

And then he said something that has echoed for two and a half thousand years. The unexamined life, he told the jury, is not worth living.

They found him guilty. The vote was close — 280 to 220. Under Athenian law, he could have proposed a lesser punishment. Exile, perhaps. A fine. His friends begged him to. Instead, in what was either his finest act of principle or his most infuriating act of stubbornness, he suggested that Athens should reward him with free meals for life, as it did for its Olympic athletes, because he had done the city a greater service than any of them.

The jury, unamused, sentenced him to death.

He was given hemlock — a poison that kills slowly, from the feet upward, numbing the body in stages until it reaches the heart. His friends wept. Socrates, according to Plato, spent his final hours doing what he had spent his life doing. He asked questions. About death. About what comes after. About whether there was any reason to fear it. He drank the poison, walked around until his legs grew heavy, lay down, and died.

Athens had silenced its most dangerous citizen. The man who knew nothing, and would not stop asking why, was gone.

But the questions were not.

CHAPTER 1.2

THE LAST HUMAN ADVANTAGE

For almost all of human history, answers were the scarce resource and questions were cheap. If you wanted to know how far it was from London to Constantinople, you had to find someone who had made the journey, or locate a rare and expensive book, or simply not know. If you wanted to understand why the sky was blue, you needed access to a natural philosopher, a university, a library — institutions that most people on Earth would never encounter. Knowledge was locked behind walls of geography, wealth, language, and time. The person who held the answer held the power.

Every major institution in human civilisation was built on this scarcity. Universities exist because knowledge needed to be gathered in one place and transmitted by experts. Libraries exist because books were rare and needed to be preserved. Professions — law, medicine, engineering, finance — exist because specialised knowledge was difficult to acquire and therefore valuable. The entire architecture of education, from primary school to postgraduate research, is designed for a world in which the fundamental problem is: how do we get the right answer to the person who needs it?

That world is gone.

It did not decline gradually. It collapsed, almost overnight, in historical terms. The internet made answers accessible. Search engines made them findable. And now, artificial intelligence has made them generative — you do not even need to know where to look, because the machine will construct the answer for you, tailored to your specific question, in seconds, in any language, at any level of complexity you request, for free.

The entire structure of scarcity that gave answers their value has evaporated. And if you are paying attention, the implications are vertiginous. If answers are no longer scarce, then the institutions built on their scarcity are standing on a foundation that has quietly disappeared. The university that charges you a hundred thousand dollars to access knowledge that is now freely available. The lawyer who bills by the hour for research a machine can do in moments. The doctor whose diagnostic authority rests on years of memorised knowledge that an AI can now match. These are not broken institutions. They are institutions designed for a world that no longer exists, and they have not yet noticed.

But here is where Socrates reaches across twenty-five centuries and grabs you by the collar. If answers are now unlimited, instant, and free, then what is the scarce resource? What holds value in a world drowning in information?

The question does.

Think about your own experience with AI. You have almost certainly typed a question into a chatbot or search engine and received an answer that was technically correct but useless — because you had asked the wrong question. The machine gave you exactly what you requested and it was not what you needed. You have also, perhaps, had the opposite experience: you asked a precise, carefully framed question and received an answer that unlocked something genuinely valuable. The difference between these two experiences was not the quality of the machine. It was the quality of the question.

This is the Socratic revolution applied to the twenty-first century. In a world of infinite answers, the question is everything. The person who asks the right question — the one that cuts through noise, that reframes a problem, that opens a door no one else noticed — holds more power than the person who holds a million answers. Because the answers are already there. They are waiting. The only thing missing is someone who knows what to ask.

And yet. Look at how the world is responding to this shift. Schools still train students to produce answers. Exams still reward the person who can recall facts under time pressure. Job interviews still favour the candidate who can demonstrate what they know, not what they would ask. The entire machinery of credentialing, from kindergarten to the C-suite, is calibrated for a world in which knowing things was the hard part.

Socrates would have found this baffling. He spent his life demonstrating that confident answers were the most dangerous things in the world — not because answers are bad, but because an answer you have not questioned is an answer you do not actually understand. The general who cannot define courage does not truly possess it. The politician who cannot define justice cannot truly serve it. The student who can recite a fact but cannot interrogate it has memorised a sound, not grasped a truth.

What Socrates understood, and what the age of AI is about to force everyone to confront, is that the quality of your thinking is not determined by how much you know. It is determined by how well you question what you know. And this is not a skill that most people have been taught. It is, in fact, a skill that most education systems have actively suppressed, because questioning is disruptive, uncomfortable, and very hard to grade.

The Socratic method — the relentless, patient, sometimes infuriating practice of asking why, and then asking why again, and then asking why the answer to why is what it is — is not a relic of ancient philosophy. It is the operating system for an age in which answers are infinite and discernment is everything. The person who can question effectively — who can interrogate an AI's output, challenge a consensus, reframe a problem, and ask the question no one else thought to ask — is the person who will navigate this world. Everyone else will be navigated.

CHAPTER 1.3

WHAT HAPPENS WHEN NOBODY ASKS?

Socrates died for a habit that his city found intolerable: he would not stop asking questions. Athens wanted certainty, stability, and the comfort of unchallenged authority. Socrates offered doubt, disruption, and the relentless insistence that nothing should be believed simply because someone powerful said it was true. The city chose to kill him rather than tolerate the discomfort of his inquiries.

Twenty-five centuries later, the tension Socrates embodied has not resolved. It has intensified. The world now produces more answers in a single day than all the scholars of ancient Athens encountered in their lifetimes. AI systems generate explanations, analyses, recommendations, and solutions with a fluency that can feel, to the unprepared, like omniscience. The temptation to stop asking — to simply accept the output, trust the algorithm, defer to the machine — has never been greater.

What happens next is not certain. But two directions are visible, and the lesson of Socrates holds in both.

The Brighter Horizon

In this future, questions become the most valued currency in the world, and people finally build the institutions to match.

Education undergoes its deepest transformation since the invention of the printing press. Schools stop testing what students can remember and start cultivating what they can ask. A child is no longer evaluated on whether they can produce the correct answer to a mathematical problem — the machine does that instantly. They are evaluated on whether they can identify the right problem to solve. The best students are not the ones who know the most. They are the ones who notice the gap, the inconsistency, the unasked question hiding in plain sight.

Professions reorganise around inquiry rather than expertise. A doctor's most valuable skill is no longer diagnosis — AI handles the pattern-matching. It is the ability to ask the patient the question they did not know they needed to answer: not what are your symptoms, but what are you afraid of? A lawyer's edge is not legal research but the capacity to reframe a conflict so that resolution becomes visible. A business leader's worth is measured not by their ability to make decisions but by their ability to ask the question that changes which decisions are available.

In this world, AI becomes what the Oracle at Delphi was for Socrates — not a source of final truth, but a provocation. A starting point for deeper inquiry. The wisest users of AI are not the ones who accept its answers. They are the ones who know how to question them: to probe for assumptions, test for blind spots, and push the machine toward territory it did not know it could reach. The Socratic method, born in an open marketplace in Athens, becomes the foundational skill of the most powerful civilisation in history.

The Darker Horizon

In this future, the age of answers wins. And the cost is everything Socrates warned us about.

The machine answers before the question is fully formed. AI systems, trained on your history, your preferences, your patterns, begin to predict what you want to know and deliver it before you ask. The experience is seamless, frictionless, and deeply satisfying. It is also the end of curiosity.

When answers arrive before questions, the muscle of inquiry atrophies. You stop wondering, because the wondering has been done for you. You stop challenging, because the output is so fluent, so confident, so precisely calibrated to your expectations, that challenging it feels unnecessary. The general cannot define courage — but it no longer matters, because the machine defines it for him, and the definition sounds right, and he has lost the habit of checking.

A new kind of ignorance emerges. Not the old kind — the absence of information. A new kind: the absence of doubt. People know everything and question nothing. They hold vast amounts of information, supplied effortlessly by machines, and almost none of it has been tested by their own thinking. They are, in Socrates's terms, the most dangerous kind of person: the ones who believe they understand things they have never examined.

In this world, power concentrates not in the hands of those who ask, but in the hands of those who design the systems that answer. The people who build the algorithms decide which questions get surfaced and which get suppressed, which perspectives get amplified and which get buried. If Socrates were alive in this future, he would not be put on trial. He would be irrelevant. The marketplace where questions once rang out has been replaced by a feed that already knows what you want to hear.

The distance between these two futures is not measured in technology. It is measured in a habit of mind — one that a barefoot stonemason's son practised in the streets of Athens until the city could no longer stand it.

Socrates could not give you the answer. That was the whole point. He could only give you the question, and the discomfort that comes with realising that your certainty was thinner than you thought. That discomfort is not a flaw. It is the engine. It is the thing that separates a mind that is alive from a mind that is merely full.

In the age of AI, every answer you need is available. The question is whether you still have the instinct to question it — and the courage not to stop.

But a question, no matter how powerful, is only as good as the mind that holds it. And a mind can only hold a question properly if it is fully present — undistracted, unscattered, awake to the thing in front of it. Socrates practised this naturally. He could stand in one spot for hours, lost in a single thought, oblivious to everything around him. The next story is about someone who turned that kind of focus into something far more visceral — and far more dangerous. A man who proved that the ability to be completely, devastatingly present is not a philosophy. It is a weapon.

2. Miyamoto Musashi

Miyamoto Musashi was the author of the Five Rings, the classic treatise on living the samurai way. This is a statue of him at his grave.

CHAPTER 2.1

THE SWORD THAT DIDN'T MOVE

In the early seventeenth century, Japan was a country that had been at war with itself for over a hundred years. The Sengoku period — the Age of Warring States — had shattered the old order. Warlords fought warlords. Alliances formed and dissolved like weather. Castles rose and burned. Entire provinces changed hands in a season. In this world, the sword was not a metaphor. It was the most immediate, most consequential tool a person could possess. A skilled swordsman could earn a lord's patronage, command a retinue, build a name. An unskilled one was simply dead.

Swordsmanship in Japan was not treated as a trade. It was treated as a path — a discipline that engaged the body, the mind, and something harder to name. The great sword schools did not just teach technique. They taught perception, timing, composure under pressure, the ability to read an opponent's intention before it became action. A duel between masters was not a contest of strength. It was a contest of awareness. The man who saw more clearly, who perceived the opening a fraction of a second before it appeared, won. The other man died.

Into this world, in 1584, in the village of Miyamoto in Harima Province, a boy was born who would become the most celebrated swordsman in Japanese history. His name was Shinmen Musashi no Kami Fujiwara no Genshin. History remembers him as Miyamoto Musashi. He would fight over sixty duels across his lifetime and never lose a single one.

What made him extraordinary was not what you would expect.

He did not come from privilege. His father, Shinmen Munisai, was a martial artist of some local renown, but the household was harsh. Musashi's mother died when he was young. His father was violent, possibly abusive, and largely absent. By the age of seven, Musashi was essentially raised by his uncle, a Buddhist monk. He grew into an oversized, unkempt, socially difficult teenager — the kind of boy that other children instinctively avoided and adults regarded with unease.

At thirteen, he killed a man. A travelling martial artist named Arima Kihei had posted a public challenge in the village, inviting anyone to face him. Musashi, barely adolescent, showed up with a wooden stick. Kihei was an experienced adult fighter with a real sword. Musashi threw him to the ground and beat him to death.

The accounts are blunt about this. There was no elegance. It was the violence of a feral boy with extraordinary reflexes and no fear whatsoever.

For the next fifteen years, Musashi wandered Japan, fighting. He challenged every school, every master, every reputation he could find. He fought with swords, with wooden weapons, with improvised tools. He fought multiple opponents at once. He fought in rain, on bridges, in temple grounds. He accumulated victories the way other men accumulated debts — relentlessly, almost compulsively. By his late twenties, he was the most feared duelist in Japan, and also one of the least understood. Because the more he fought, the less his victories looked like fighting.

The duel that defined his legend took place on the 13th of April, 1612, on a small tidal island called Ganryu, in the strait between Honshu and Kyushu. His opponent was Sasaki Kojiro — a swordsman whose technique was considered the most refined in the country. Kojiro had developed a signature strike called the Tsubame Gaeshi, the Swallow Cut, named for the way a swallow reverses direction in flight. It was fast, deceptive, and reportedly unbeatable. Kojiro served a powerful lord. He had a formal school, devoted students, and an impeccable reputation. By every conventional measure, he was the superior fighter.

The duel was scheduled for the morning. Kojiro arrived at the island at the appointed time, dressed immaculately, carrying a long sword of exceptional quality. He waited. The morning wore on. Musashi did not appear. An hour passed. Then another. Kojiro paced the beach. His seconds grew restless. The tide shifted. Still no Musashi.

He was asleep. Or rather, he had overslept — deliberately, most historians believe, though some accounts suggest he was simply indifferent to the schedule. When he finally roused himself and boarded the boat to Ganryu Island, he did something that would have struck any formal swordsman as either insane or insulting. He took a spare oar from the boat and, as the ferryman rowed, carved it into a rough wooden sword with a knife. He did not bring his own weapon. He fashioned one from a piece of the boat.

He arrived at the island hours late, dishevelled, carrying a crude wooden paddle. Kojiro was furious. His composure — the precise, cultivated calm that underpinned his technique — was cracking. He had been standing on a beach for hours, in full ceremonial readiness, watching the tide change, and his opponent had shown up looking like a man who had wandered in from a fishing trip.

What happened next lasted seconds. Kojiro drew his sword and threw his scabbard into the sand. Musashi reportedly said: you will not be needing that again. Kojiro charged. Musashi stepped forward with the wooden oar and struck once. Kojiro fell. One blow. The most technically gifted swordsman in Japan, wielding a finely forged blade, was defeated by a man with a boat oar who could not be bothered to arrive on time.

This is the story the legends love. The dramatic lateness. The wooden sword. The single strike. But the legends usually miss the point. Musashi did not win because he was faster, or stronger, or more technically skilled. Kojiro was almost certainly his equal in pure technique and possibly his superior. Musashi won because, by the time the duel began, it was already over.

The lateness was not rudeness. It was strategy — but not the crude kind. Musashi did not simply want to annoy his opponent. He wanted to occupy his opponent's mind. Every minute Kojiro waited on that beach, his attention divided. Part of him was preparing for the duel. Part of him was wondering where Musashi was. Part of him was growing angry. Part of him was managing the anger. By the time Musashi stepped off the boat, Kojiro's mind was a crowded room. Musashi's was empty.

The wooden sword was the same principle applied differently. It was an insult that Kojiro could not ignore. It said: you are not dangerous enough for me to bring a real weapon. Whether Kojiro believed this or not was irrelevant. The thought was in his head. It was taking up space. Another distraction, another fracture in the perfect composure that his technique required.

And the scabbard. When Kojiro threw his scabbard on the sand — a gesture of commitment, an experienced fighter's ritual — Musashi read it as a signal of agitation, of a man who had abandoned the calm centre from which precise action flows. The comment about not needing it again was not bravado. It was a diagnosis.

Musashi saw all of this because he was present in a way that Kojiro was not. His mind held nothing but the moment: the distance between them, the angle of the light, the weight of the oar, the shift in Kojiro's stance. There was no anger in him, no anxiety, no narrative about what should be happening. There was only what was happening. And what was happening, to a mind that clear, was obvious.

After Ganryu Island, Musashi never fought another serious duel. He spent the remaining thirty years of his life pursuing what he had glimpsed in those brief, violent encounters: the nature of perception itself. He studied painting — ink wash and calligraphy, disciplines that demand the same acute awareness of the present moment. He sculpted. He wrote. He became, in the decades after his fighting career, one of the most accomplished artists in Japanese history.

In the final weeks of his life, living in a cave called Reigando on the outskirts of Kumamoto, Musashi wrote a slim book called Go Rin No Sho — The Book of Five Rings. It is ostensibly a manual on swordsmanship. It is actually a treatise on perception. On seeing things as they are, rather than as you expect them to be, or fear them to be, or wish them to be. On the difference between looking and seeing. On the cultivation of a mind so completely present that nothing — no emotion, no expectation, no distraction — stands between it and reality.

He called this the gaze of two eyes — the ability to see simultaneously the surface of things and the truth beneath them. It was not mysticism. It was not meditation in the abstract sense. It was a practical, hard-won discipline built across sixty-one duels and thirty years of art: the discipline of being entirely, ferociously here.

Musashi died in 1645, in his cave, having traded a life of violence for a life of attention. The greatest swordsman in Japanese history had discovered that his real weapon was never the sword. It was the quality of his awareness. Everything else was just an instrument.

CHAPTER 2.2

THE ATTENTION WAR

You are currently losing a war that you did not agree to fight, against an opponent you cannot see, over a resource you did not know you had. The resource is your attention. And it is the most valuable thing you possess.

This is not hyperbole. Every hour of your waking life, an infrastructure of extraordinary sophistication is working to capture, hold, and monetise the contents of your awareness. The notification that just lit up your phone was not sent because you needed to see it. It was sent because your glance is worth money. The video that auto-played as you scrolled was not selected because it was good. It was selected because the algorithm calculated, based on thousands of data points, that it would hold your eyes for seven more seconds. The news headline that made your stomach clench was not written to inform you. It was written to make you click, because your click is a unit of currency in an economy that trades in human attention.

This is the world Musashi would have recognised instantly. Not the technology — the dynamic. A battle for perception. A contest in which the winner is the party that controls where awareness is directed, and the loser is the party that does not realise their awareness is being directed at all.

Musashi understood something about presence that neuroscience is only now confirming: attention is not just a mental preference. It is a biological state. When you are fully present — when your entire cognitive apparatus is focused on a single point of reality — the brain operates differently. Perception sharpens. Pattern recognition accelerates. The noise of anxiety, rumination, and distraction falls away, and what remains is a startling clarity about what is actually in front of you.

Athletes call this the zone. Musicians call it flow. Musashi called it no-mind — not the absence of thought, but the absence of interference. A mind so present that it does not add a layer of interpretation between itself and reality. It does not say this is dangerous before it perceives the danger. It does not say I should be worried before it identifies what to be worried about. It simply sees. And in that seeing, the appropriate response arises on its own, faster and more accurate than any conscious deliberation could produce.

On Ganryu Island, this is what gave Musashi his edge. Kojiro was distracted — by anger, by the insult of the wooden sword, by hours of waiting, by the narrative in his head about what should have happened and what it meant that it hadn't. Every one of those thoughts was a fraction of a second of delay between perception and action. In a sword fight, fractions of a second are the difference between life and death. Musashi had no such delays. He saw the strike, the opening, the angle of resolution, and his body moved. There was nothing between the seeing and the doing. Nothing.

Now consider your own day. How many minutes of it are spent in that state of clarity? How many hours pass in which your awareness is genuinely, fully directed at the thing in front of you — not the thing your phone is suggesting, not the conversation you had this morning, not the worry about tomorrow, but the actual present moment?

The honest answer, for most people, is almost none. And this is not because you are weak-willed or undisciplined. It is because you are living inside a machine that has been specifically, brilliantly engineered to prevent exactly this state. The attention economy does not want you present. It wants you fragmented. A fragmented mind clicks more, scrolls more, consumes more. A present mind closes the app and looks at the sky. The first is worth billions. The second is worth nothing — to the economy.

To you, of course, it is worth everything. The quality of your relationships depends on your ability to be present with another person. The quality of your work depends on your ability to hold a complex problem in your mind without distraction. The quality of your decisions depends on your ability to see the situation clearly, without the noise of anxiety or the fog of fragmented attention. Presence is not a luxury. It is the foundation on which every other human capacity rests.

And it is eroding.

Here is the connection to AI that most people miss. The conversation about artificial intelligence tends to focus on capability: what can AI do, and will it do it better than us? These are important questions. But they are not the most urgent ones. The most urgent question is not what can AI do. It is what is AI doing to the quality of your attention?

Because an AI system, no matter how powerful, does not replace your thinking. It augments it or it degrades it, and the difference depends entirely on the quality of the mind that engages with it. If you bring a distracted, fragmented, half-present mind to a conversation with AI, you will get distracted, fragmented, half-useful results. You will accept the first output. You will not notice the assumption buried in the response. You will not think to reframe the question. The machine will have done its job. Your mind will not have done yours.

If you bring a present mind — one that is fully engaged, aware of what it is asking and why, capable of recognising the gap between what was requested and what was delivered — the same machine becomes an entirely different tool. Not a replacement for thought, but an amplifier of it. The difference is not in the machine. It is in you.

Musashi would have understood this immediately. The sword is the same for both fighters. The difference is in the eye that guides it.

CHAPTER 2.3

THE LAST THING MACHINES CAN'T SIMULATE

Musashi spent sixty-one duels discovering that the decisive advantage in any contest is not skill, not strength, not strategy, but the quality of awareness you bring to the moment. Everything else is downstream of that. The better you see, the better you act. The more present you are, the less noise stands between you and reality.

This principle is about to be tested at a scale Musashi could not have imagined. AI is evolving at a pace that makes yesterday's capabilities look quaint. What does not evolve — what shows no sign of evolving — is AI's capacity for presence. A machine can process, predict, generate, and optimise. But it cannot be here. It cannot experience the texture of a moment, the weight of a silence, the shift in someone's posture that tells you more than their words. It cannot be present, because presence requires the one thing no machine possesses: the experience of being.

The future will test whether humans can protect and cultivate this capacity, or whether they will let it atrophy. Two directions are visible.

The Brighter Horizon

In this future, the crisis of attention produces its own cure. As the damage becomes undeniable — rising anxiety, collapsing attention spans, relationships hollowed out by distraction — a counter-movement grows. Not a rejection of technology, but a renegotiation with it.

People begin treating attention with the same seriousness that previous generations treated literacy. Schools teach it. Companies protect it. Individuals invest in it as deliberately as they invest in their careers or their health. The ability to focus deeply, to be fully present with a person or a problem, becomes recognised as the scarce and precious resource it has always been.

AI becomes part of the solution. Intelligent systems learn to filter rather than flood — reducing noise instead of amplifying it, protecting attention rather than exploiting it. A new generation of tools emerges that measures its value not by how much of your time it captures, but by how much of your time it gives back. Technology, designed properly, becomes the guard at the gate rather than the army at the walls.

In this world, presence becomes the defining human advantage in every field. The doctor who is truly present with a patient catches the hesitation in their voice that the diagnostic AI missed. The negotiator who is fully in the room reads the shift in posture that changes the entire strategy. The teacher who is genuinely here, in this moment, with this student, sees the spark of understanding that no algorithm could have predicted.

Musashi's insight scales from the duel to the civilisation: the mind that is fully present has an advantage that no amount of processing power can replicate.

The Darker Horizon

In this future, attention continues to fragment, and no counter-movement arrives in time.

AI-generated content becomes so perfectly personalised, so precisely calibrated to individual neurological triggers, that sustained focus becomes physiologically difficult for most people. Not impossible — but as rare and effortful as running a marathon. The capacity for deep attention, once universal, becomes a specialist skill possessed by a shrinking minority.

A new class divide emerges — not between rich and poor, or educated and uneducated, but between the focused and the fragmented. Those who can hold their attention — who can sit with a complex problem, sustain a difficult conversation, read a long argument without reaching for their phone — occupy a different cognitive tier than those who cannot. They make better decisions, build deeper relationships, produce more original work. They see what others miss, not because they are smarter, but because they are present.

The fragmented majority does not suffer from a lack of information. They suffer from a lack of coherence. They know everything and understand nothing, because understanding requires the one thing they can no longer sustain: attention held long enough for the pieces to connect. Their lives are a stream of stimuli without a narrative. They respond to everything and reflect on nothing.

In this world, Musashi's lesson becomes a parable about what was lost. The man who could empty his mind and see clearly — who could stand on a beach with nothing between himself and reality — becomes a figure from a world as distant and incomprehensible as the samurai era itself.

The distance between these futures is not measured in decades. It is measured in the daily decisions you make about where your attention goes. Every time you choose to be present — with a person, with a problem, with the difficult silence that precedes real thought — you are choosing the brighter horizon. Every time you default to the scroll, the notification, the frictionless consumption of content you did not choose and will not remember, you are choosing the other one.

Musashi spent a lifetime refining his ability to see clearly in the midst of chaos. He did not achieve it naturally. He achieved it through practice, failure, and the kind of discipline that looks, from the outside, like obsession. But the result was a man who could walk onto a beach with a wooden oar and defeat the finest swordsman in Japan, because he was the only one in the fight who was actually there.

The question for you is not whether you are as disciplined as Musashi. Nobody is asking you to be. The question is simpler and more uncomfortable: in the last hour, were you fully present for any of it?

Socrates taught us to question. Musashi taught us to see. But what happens when what you see — when the truth that your clear, present, questioning mind arrives at — contradicts everything you have been taught, everything your community believes, everything your identity is built on? What do you do when being present means confronting a reality you desperately wish were not true?

The next story is about a man who faced exactly this. A quiet administrator in a small town in Poland, who pointed his mathematics at the sky and discovered that the universe was not what anyone thought it was. The truth he found was so dangerous that he hid it for thirty years. And when he finally let it go, it changed everything.

3. Copernicus

The statue in Warsaw, opposite the Academy of Sciences

CHAPTER 3.1

THE MAN WHO MOVED THE EARTH

If you had stood outside on a clear night in early sixteenth-century Europe and looked up, you would have seen something entirely different from what you see today. Not because the sky was different. Because you were.

You would have seen a ceiling. A vast, glittering, sacred ceiling, stretched over the Earth by God himself and studded with lights that existed for a single purpose: you. The stars were not distant suns. They were decorations — fixed points of light embedded in a crystalline sphere that marked the outermost boundary of creation. Beyond that sphere lay Heaven. Below it, nested inside it like the layers of an onion, seven more spheres carried the Moon, the Sun, and the five known planets in perfect, eternal circles around the Earth.

The Earth did not move. This was not a theory. It was as obvious as breathing. You could feel the ground beneath your feet, solid and still. You watched the Sun rise in the east and set in the west, obediently tracing its path around you, because you were the point. You were why all of this existed. The entire architecture of the cosmos — from the sphere of the Moon to the throne of God — was built around the place where you were standing.

This was the universe as understood by Ptolemy, the Greco-Egyptian astronomer who had codified the model in the second century, and it had stood, essentially unchallenged, for fourteen hundred years. Not because people were incurious. Because the model worked. It predicted eclipses. It mapped the movements of the planets with reasonable accuracy. Sailors navigated by it. Farmers planted by it. The Church built its theology on it. And if you had told anyone — a bishop, a professor, a merchant, a fisherman — that the Earth was actually spinning at a thousand miles per hour while hurtling through space around the Sun, they would not have argued with you. They would have worried for your sanity.

There was, however, one persistent annoyance. Every now and then, a planet would appear to slow down, stop, and drift backwards across the night sky for a few weeks before resuming its forward course. Mars did this. Jupiter did this. If the planets were embedded in rotating crystalline spheres, this should have been impossible. A sphere cannot suddenly change its mind.

The solution was ingenious. Astronomers proposed that each planet did not simply orbit the Earth in one large circle. It also traced a smaller circle as it went — a loop within the loop. Picture a child sitting on a carousel that is itself mounted on a larger carousel. From the ground, the child's path looks mostly smooth. But at certain moments, the smaller rotation carries the child briefly backward relative to the larger one. These smaller loops were called epicycles, and they were clever. They explained the backward drift. They saved the model.

And then they bred. As observations improved over the centuries, each new discrepancy required another adjustment — a loop on top of a loop, a patch stitched onto a patch. By the early 1500s, the model needed roughly eighty of these corrections to match what astronomers actually saw in the sky. The elegant machine Ptolemy had built now looked like something held together with faith and string. It still predicted. It still functioned. But it had lost the one quality that should worry you when it disappears from a system meant to describe the truth: simplicity.

Nicolaus Copernicus was the last person you would expect to tear this structure apart. He was a canon of the Catholic Church — not a priest, but an administrator, collecting rents and managing finances for the cathedral chapter in Frauenburg, a town in northern Poland so small and remote that most Europeans could not have found it on a map. He lived in a tower attached to the cathedral wall. He practised medicine on the side, treating the local clergy and townspeople. He ate meals with other canons, attended services, and observed the routines of a quiet, institutional life. He was, by every surviving account, a man who valued order, avoided confrontation, and had no appetite whatsoever for revolution.

He had studied astronomy in Italy as a young man, and he was gifted — meticulous, patient, and possessed of the kind of mathematical sensibility that experiences an ugly equation the way a musician experiences a wrong note. When the Church needed its calendar fixed — Easter was slowly sliding out of alignment with the spring equinox — Copernicus was the sort of capable, reliable person who would be asked to help.

So he sat down with Ptolemy's model and tried to make the numbers exact. He refined observations. He tightened calculations. And the numbers, stubbornly, beautifully, catastrophically, refused to cooperate. The more precisely he modelled planetary motion with the Earth at the centre, the more corrections the system demanded. The architecture groaned. The patches needed patches.

And then he did the thing that changed everything. Not as a declaration. Not as an act of defiance. As a quiet experiment — the guilty, half-hoping-it-won't-work kind. He took the Earth out of the centre and put the Sun there. He made the Earth a planet, orbiting the Sun alongside the others.

The mathematics transformed. The backward motion of the planets vanished. It had never been real — it was an illusion created by the Earth itself moving, overtaking slower outer planets in its orbit the way a faster car seems to push a slower one backward as it passes. The loops within loops, the eighty corrections, the centuries of desperate patching — most of them simply fell away. The model breathed. For the first time since Ptolemy, the heavens looked clean.

And Copernicus understood, with a horror that would shadow the rest of his life, exactly what he had done.

Placing the Sun at the centre was not a correction. It was an act of destruction aimed at the deepest conviction his civilisation held about itself.

The medieval cosmos was not just an astronomical model. It was a moral architecture. The Earth sat at the centre because humanity sat at the centre. Humanity sat at the centre because God had placed it there — the point of creation, the audience for whom the entire cosmic theatre had been staged. The spheres orbited us because we were the reason they existed. Remove the Earth from the centre, and you did not rearrange the furniture. You pulled the floor out from under every cathedral, every prayer, every assumption about why the universe existed and who it existed for.

Copernicus saw this chain of implications with terrible clarity. He was not a fool. He was an employee of the institution whose entire authority rested on the cosmology he had just disproved. He ate its bread. He slept inside its walls. He depended on it for his livelihood, his community, his place in the world.

And then there was the more intimate terror. He had to disbelieve his own body. Every morning, the Sun rose. Every evening, it set. The ground was firm and still. To accept his own mathematics was to accept that the most basic, most trustworthy evidence available to a human being — the evidence of direct physical experience — was a lie. Not a distortion. Not an approximation. A complete inversion of reality. The ground moves. The Sun is still. Everything your body has ever told you about where you are and what is happening is wrong.

Try to hold this for a moment. Not as a fact you learned in school and filed away. As a lived sensation. You are standing on a rock that is spinning and flying through a void at unthinkable speed, and every nerve in your body insists it is stationary. Your senses are not making a small error. They are constructing a version of reality that is the opposite of the truth. And you have to carry that knowledge quietly, alone, in a community that would be horrified if they knew.

Copernicus carried it for over thirty years.

He hid. There is no gentler way to say it. For more than three decades, Copernicus kept his heliocentric model essentially private. He shared the broad idea in a brief handwritten summary — the Commentariolus — which circulated among a small circle of trusted astronomers. But the full proof, the work that would become De Revolutionibus Orbium Coelestium, he would not release. He revised it. He fussed. He found reasons to delay. Year after year, decade after decade, the manuscript sat in his tower while its author collected rents, treated patients, and attended services in a cathedral built on the assumption that the Earth was the centre of God's creation.

He was not perfecting the work. He was hiding from it.

This is the part of Copernicus's story that makes him so achingly human. He was not a hero who boldly proclaimed the truth. He was a man who discovered something enormous, understood its consequences, and spent most of his life unable to face them. He knew that Giordano Bruno would later be burned alive for defending similar ideas, though he could not have known the specific fate. He knew the Church's capacity for punishment. He knew what happened to people who challenged the shared map. And he chose, for thirty years, to let the truth sit in a drawer.

It was a young mathematician named Georg Joachim Rheticus who finally pried the work loose. Rheticus arrived in Frauenburg in 1539, already convinced Copernicus was right, and spent two years persuading, encouraging, and ultimately arranging for publication. He shepherded the manuscript to a printer in Nuremberg. He handled the logistics that Copernicus could not bring himself to face.

The printing was completed in early 1543. A copy was sent to Frauenburg. By the time it arrived, Copernicus had suffered a stroke. He was bedridden, fading. Some accounts say the book was placed in his hands and he touched the cover before dying. Others say he never regained enough consciousness to recognise it. What is not disputed is the timing: Nicolaus Copernicus died on the 24th of May, 1543, the same day — or very nearly the same day — that the book that would rearrange the universe reached him.

Whether this was coincidence or the final act of a man who had timed his courage to expire alongside himself, no one will ever know. But the image is almost unbearable: a dying clergyman in a remote Polish town, holding in his hands the proof that everything his world believed about itself was wrong, released at the exact moment when he would never have to face what came next.

What came next was the modern world.

De Revolutionibus did not cause an immediate revolution. The Church largely ignored it for decades. Most astronomers treated it as a mathematical convenience rather than a description of reality. But the idea had been released, and ideas, once released, do not return to their towers.

Copernicus gave Galileo the framework to point a telescope at Jupiter and see four moons orbiting another planet — devastating, visible proof that not everything revolves around the Earth. Galileo gave Kepler the confidence to formulate the laws of planetary motion. Kepler gave Newton the architecture for universal gravitation. Newton gave the Enlightenment its engine. The Enlightenment gave us the scientific method, the industrial revolution, modern medicine, and the world you are living in right now.

Every major intellectual revolution since 1543 is a descendant of a frightened church administrator who could not make the numbers work and was honest enough — just barely, just fatally honest enough — to say so.

It all began with a man who unlearned the centre of the universe. And the unlearning has not stopped since.

CHAPTER 3.2

WHY LETTING GO IS THE HARDEST HUMAN ACT

Every person alive carries a private map of reality inside their head. It was assembled over years from what you were taught, what you experienced, what the people around you seemed to agree on, and what simply felt true. Most of this map was drawn before you were old enough to question it. By the time you could, the map had already hardened into something that no longer felt like a map at all. It felt like the world itself.

This is what makes unlearning so different from learning. Learning is addition. You build, you expand, you layer new understanding on top of what you already hold. It feels like growth, and human beings enjoy growth. Unlearning is demolition. It asks you to reach into the architecture of your own understanding and pull out a load-bearing wall — one that you may have built your career on, your relationships around, your sense of self upon — without knowing whether the structure will survive.

That is not a minor disruption. That is an earthquake in the foundations of who you believe yourself to be. And every person who has ever truly unlearned something will recognise the three distinct tremors that Copernicus experienced — because they are not historical curiosities. They are universal human patterns.

The first tremor is the betrayal of experience. You trust your senses. You have to — they are the most immediate, most intimate source of information you possess. When your eyes tell you the Sun is moving across the sky, that information arrives with the full authority of physical reality behind it. It is not a theory. It is not an argument. It is the sky, right there, doing the thing. To unlearn this kind of knowledge is to accept that your body — the instrument you have relied on for every moment of your existence — has been feeding you a version of reality that is not just incomplete but inverted. The Sun is still. The ground moves. And you cannot feel any of it.

This is why people resist unlearning even when the evidence is overwhelming. It is not stupidity. It is not stubbornness, at least not the ordinary kind. It is the deep, primal terror of discovering that the tool you use to perceive reality is unreliable. If your senses were wrong about this, what else have they been wrong about? The ground shifts, and once it shifts, it does not stop shifting.

The second tremor is the collapse of identity. Your beliefs are not accessories. They are not things you carry around and swap out when a more fashionable option appears. They are structural. They are woven into who you are — into how you introduce yourself, how you make decisions, how you understand your place among other people. Ask someone to change their mind about something that sits at the core of their identity, and you are not asking for an intellectual update. You are asking them to demolish a piece of who they are and build something new in the wreckage, with no guarantee that the new construction will hold.

When a doctor who has spent fifteen years mastering diagnostic medicine encounters an AI system that matches their accuracy in minutes, the threat is not professional. It is existential. The story they tell themselves about who they are and why they matter is built on the foundation of a skill that is being made ordinary. When a teacher discovers that their students can get clearer explanations from a chatbot than from their lecture, the crisis is not pedagogical. It is an assault on the structure of their self-understanding. It strikes at the centre of what they believed made them valuable.

Copernicus faced this in its purest form. He was not merely a man with astronomical opinions. He was a servant of the Church, and the Church's authority rested on the cosmology he had disproved. To publish was not to correct an error. It was to detonate the foundation of the institution that gave his life its structure, its community, its meaning. Imagine tearing down the house you live in while you are still standing inside it. Now imagine that the house belongs to the most powerful institution in Europe, and it does not take kindly to demolition.

The third tremor is social. No belief is held alone. Every conviction you carry is reinforced by the people around you who carry the same one. Your community, your profession, your culture — these are not just groups you belong to. They are agreements. Shared maps of reality that make cooperation, conversation, and trust possible. When you unlearn something that your community still holds to be true, you do not simply change your mind. You break the agreement. And the community's response, almost without exception, is not to update the map. It is to punish the mapmaker.

Copernicus knew this. Giordano Bruno would be burned alive in 1600 for defending ideas that followed from heliocentrism. Galileo would spend his final years under house arrest. The consequences of stepping outside the shared map were not abstract. They were physical, public, and terrifying.

This is the deepest reason Copernicus hid for thirty years. Not cowardice in the simple sense. Something more painful: the recognition that unlearning is never a private act. The moment you speak what you have discovered, you force everyone who hears it to confront their own map. And most people, when their map is threatened, do not redraw it. They destroy the person who showed them it was wrong.

Now turn to the world you are living in, and notice how familiar these tremors feel.

For roughly two hundred thousand years, Homo sapiens has held an assumption so deep it barely registers as an assumption at all. It is more like gravity — so fundamental that questioning it feels faintly ridiculous. The assumption is this: humans are the intelligent species. We are the thinkers. The creators. The problem-solvers. Everything else — every animal, every tool, every machine — exists below us on a hierarchy that we defined, and we defined it by placing ourselves at the top.

This assumption is the geocentric model of the mind. It places human cognition at the centre of everything. It organises our education, our economies, our legal structures, and our sense of purpose. It tells us a doctor is valuable because no machine can do what they do. That a lawyer's judgment is worth four hundred dollars an hour because it cannot be replicated. That an artist's creativity is sacred because it is uniquely, irreducibly human.

These are not just professional claims. They are identity claims. They are the crystalline spheres of our cognitive cosmos. And they are now accumulating epicycles at an alarming rate. Why does it take twelve years to train a doctor when an AI can match their diagnostic accuracy in certain domains after a few months of data? Why do legal systems charge by the hour for contract review that a machine completes in seconds? Why do schools still test memorisation when every fact is retrievable in a heartbeat? The patches are multiplying. The model still functions. But anyone paying attention can hear it groaning under its own weight.

What AI is doing to human self-understanding is precisely what Copernicus did to the medieval cosmos. It is not correcting a detail. It is displacing us from the centre. Not the centre of space this time, but the centre of thought. And the displacement carries the same three tremors. Your direct experience still tells you that you are the smartest being in the room. Your identity is built on the assumption that your mind is special. And your community has agreed on a shared map that places human cognition at the top.

Every one of these is being shaken. Some of them have already cracked.

The Copernican lesson is not that unlearning is easy, or that it should be. It is that unlearning is the prerequisite to every major advance in human understanding. Copernicus could not fix the calendar without unfixing the cosmos. You cannot navigate the age of AI without unfixing the assumption that human intelligence is the measure of all things. The question is not whether this unlearning will happen. It will. Once the mathematics are clear, no amount of hiding, delaying, or institutional resistance can keep the old model alive forever.

The question is whether you will unlearn deliberately — with the painful, honest courage of a man who spent thirty years gathering the nerve — or whether the unlearning will be done to you, by a world that has already moved on.

CHAPTER 3.3

THE NEXT COPERNICAN SHIFT

Copernicus hid his truth for thirty years because he could see where it led, and the destination frightened him. He had, at least, the luxury of delay. The Earth had been at the centre for fourteen centuries. A few more decades of silence would not change the mathematics. The truth could wait.

You do not have that luxury. The displacement that AI is bringing to human cognition is arriving faster than any paradigm shift in history, and it will not wait politely while you decide whether to accept it. No one can predict the exact shape of what comes next — the future is not a destination but a landscape, shaped by forces too numerous and too human to forecast with certainty. But we can stand at the fault lines and look in both directions. In one direction lies a future where the unlearning goes well. In the other, a future where it does not.

In both directions, the lesson of Copernicus holds. In both, unlearning is the price of survival.

The Brighter Horizon

Imagine a future in which humanity does what it has done, eventually, after every Copernican moment in its past: it lets go of the old centre and discovers that what lies beyond it is larger, stranger, and more wondrous than what was lost.

In this future, the realisation that human intelligence is not unique does not diminish humanity. It liberates it. For centuries, we have measured our worth by our cognitive output — by how much we know, how fast we think, how cleverly we solve. We have built entire civilisations around the idea that the thinking mind is the highest expression of human value. When that pedestal is removed, something extraordinary becomes possible. We are forced to ask a question we have been avoiding for all of recorded history: if thinking is not what makes us special, then what does?

And the answers that surface are older, deeper, and more honest than anything the age of reason produced. Perhaps what makes us human was never intelligence. Perhaps it is consciousness — the raw, irreducible experience of being alive, of feeling grief, of laughing at something that is not efficient or optimal but simply funny. Perhaps it is the capacity to find meaning in a universe that offers none — to look at a sunset and feel something that no amount of processing power can replicate, because the feeling is not a computation. It is an experience. And experiences do not belong to machines.

In this future, education transforms. Schools stop training people to be warehouses of information — a function that machines now perform effortlessly — and start cultivating what no algorithm can: the ability to ask questions that have never been asked, to sit with uncertainty without flinching, to understand another human being not through data but through genuine attention. Professions evolve. The doctor's role shifts from diagnostician to meaning-maker — helping a frightened person understand what an illness means for their life, their family, their fear of death. The teacher becomes not a transmitter of facts but a cultivator of minds that can think for themselves.

The Copernican displacement, in this version, does not destroy human purpose. It purifies it. Just as removing the Earth from the centre of the cosmos eventually gave us a universe far more vast and astonishing than the medieval model could contain, removing human intelligence from the centre of cognition opens a space for something larger. A deeper reckoning with what it means to be the kind of creature that can lose its centrality and still find reasons to go on.

The Darker Horizon

But there is another direction. And intellectual honesty demands acknowledging that this direction is, historically, the more common one.

The Catholic Church did not accept Copernicus's model until 1835. That is two hundred and ninety-two years. Nearly three centuries in which the most powerful institution in Europe officially maintained a cosmology that its own astronomers had quietly abandoned. Three centuries of insisting that the old centre still held, not because the evidence supported it, but because the institution's authority depended on it.

In this darker future, the same pattern repeats. Institutions resist. Education systems continue to teach as though human cognition is supreme, producing graduates trained for a world that has already disappeared. Legal systems erect regulatory barriers to slow AI adoption — not to protect people, but to protect the professions that bill for services machines can perform in seconds. Corporations publicly celebrate human creativity while quietly replacing it. Governments issue reassuring statements about the irreplaceable value of human workers while the economic ground shifts beneath everyone's feet.

The unlearning does not happen. Not because the evidence is unclear, but because the cost of accepting it is too high for the people who benefit from the current arrangement. Every institution has its own version of the geocentric model at its foundation — a core assumption about human centrality that justifies its existence, its pricing, its claim to authority. To accept that the centre has moved is to accept that the institution itself must fundamentally change. And institutions do not change until the pain of staying the same exceeds the pain of transformation. By then, the damage is already done.

A divide opens. On one side, individuals and communities that find the courage to unlearn — who accept the displacement, grieve what is lost, and begin building identities around what remains. On the other, those who cling to the old model with increasing desperation, constructing ever more elaborate epicycles to explain why this time is different, why human intelligence is still supreme, why the Sun still revolves around the Earth.

You can already see this divide forming. It is visible in universities that charge the same tuition for the same curriculum as fifteen years ago, despite the fact that the information is now available to anyone. It is visible in professionals who resist AI tools not on principle but on self-preservation. It is visible in the discomfort that flickers across someone's face when you suggest that a machine might be better at a task they have spent their career mastering.

The darker horizon is not a world without AI. It is a world that refuses to unlearn in the face of AI. And the cost of that refusal, if Copernicus's story teaches us anything, is measured not in years but in generations.

The question is not which of these futures will arrive. Elements of both will. The brighter and the darker horizons will coexist — often in the same city, the same company, the same household. The question is which side of the divide you will stand on.

Copernicus's story offers no easy comfort. He was not a model of bold, decisive action. He was terrified. He hid. He delayed for thirty years and released the truth only as he was dying. His courage was real, but it was the thin, trembling, human kind — the kind that barely arrives in time.

But it did arrive. And the unlearning it set in motion has not stopped for five hundred years.

The Earth has moved again. The only question is whether you will move with it — deliberately, with your eyes open and your old maps folded away — or whether you will be carried, disoriented and clinging to a centre that is no longer there.

But unlearning, as Copernicus discovered, leaves a void. When you dismantle the model you have lived by — when you accept that you are not at the centre, that your certainties were incomplete, that the ground was never as still as it felt — what fills the empty space? What do you hold onto when the last wall comes down?

The next story is about a man who had that question answered for him in the most brutal way imaginable. Everything was taken — his name, his family, his life's work, his freedom, his body's autonomy. And in the wreckage, stripped to nothing, he found the one thing that could not be taken. The one thing that turned out to be the only thing that ever mattered.

ACT II

BECOME

How to Act

4. Viktor Frankl

CHAPTER 4.1

THE LAST FREEDOM

In 1942, Vienna was a city learning to forget what it had been. A decade earlier, it had been the intellectual capital of Europe — the city of Freud and Mahler, of coffeehouses where physicists argued with poets and where a young psychiatrist could walk from a lecture on the unconscious mind to a concert hall performing Brahms in twenty minutes. Vienna had produced more ideas per square mile than almost any city in history. It had also produced a particular kind of civilised confidence — the belief that culture, education, and reason formed an unbreakable floor beneath society, a foundation that could not give way.

The floor had given way. Austria had been absorbed into the Third Reich in 1938, and Vienna's Jewish population — the community that had produced a staggering proportion of its doctors, lawyers, musicians, scientists, and writers — was being systematically erased. Properties were confiscated. Businesses were seized. Neighbours who had shared meals and conversation for decades looked away, or worse. The machinery of elimination was not sudden. It was bureaucratic, methodical, and wrapped in paperwork.

Viktor Frankl was thirty-seven years old and already one of the most promising psychiatrists in the city. He ran the neurology department at Rothschild Hospital, the only medical facility still treating Jewish patients. He had developed a therapeutic approach he called logotherapy — from the Greek logos, meaning — built on a conviction that would soon be tested beyond anything he could have imagined: that the primary human drive is not pleasure, as Freud believed, or power, as Adler believed, but meaning. That a person who has a reason to endure can endure almost anything.

In 1942, Frankl received a visa to the United States. It was an escape route — the kind that hundreds of Viennese intellectuals had already used, the kind that would save his career, his work, and almost certainly his life. His bags were packed. The paperwork was complete.

And then he went home to his parents.

His father, Gabriel, was elderly and frail. His mother, Elsa, was devoted to her husband and incapable of leaving him. Neither of them had visas. Neither of them would get one. If Viktor left, he would survive. They would not. He knew this with the clarity of a man who understood exactly what the bureaucratic machinery was building toward.

He looked at the visa. He looked at his parents. And he made a decision that, by any rational calculation, was indefensible. He stayed.

Later, Frankl would describe noticing a piece of marble on his father's shelf — a fragment from a destroyed synagogue, inscribed with a portion of the Ten Commandments. The visible fragment contained part of one commandment: Honour thy father and thy mother, that thy days may be long upon the land. He took this as a sign. But it was not the sign that made the decision. The decision had already been made. The sign merely confirmed what he already knew about who he was and what his integrity required. Some doors, once walked through, cannot be un-walked. He let the visa expire.

Within months, the Frankl family was deported. Viktor, his wife Tilly, his parents, and his brother Walter were sent to Theresienstadt, a concentration camp in occupied Czechoslovakia that the Nazis maintained as a grotesque showpiece — a "model camp" presented to Red Cross inspectors while, behind the facade, prisoners starved, sickened, and were transported east to the extermination centres.

Frankl's father died at Theresienstadt. Starvation and pneumonia. Viktor was present, but there was nothing he could do — no medicine, no food, no intervention possible. He watched his father die in a place designed to make death ordinary.

In 1944, Frankl, his wife, and his mother were transferred to Auschwitz.

The selection at Auschwitz took seconds. Prisoners stepped off the cattle cars into a world that operated by a single, inhuman logic: usefulness. An SS officer glanced at each arrival and gestured — left or right. Left meant the gas chambers. Right meant forced labour, which was merely a slower form of the same sentence. Frankl was directed right. His mother was directed left. He never saw her again. Tilly was sent to Bergen-Belsen. She would not survive.

Everything Frankl had built was destroyed in a matter of hours. His career. His family. His manuscript — the book he had been writing for years, his life's intellectual work, sewn into the lining of his coat — was discovered and confiscated. His name was replaced with a number. His clothes were replaced with a striped uniform. His hair was shaved. The man who had been Dr. Viktor Frankl, psychiatrist, author, thinker, husband, son, was reduced to a body whose only value was the labour it could perform before it expired.

It is at this point that most accounts of the Holocaust become stories of endurance, of suffering described and witnessed. Frankl's story becomes something different. It becomes an experiment.

Not a deliberate one. Not one he chose. But Frankl was, even in the camps, a psychiatrist. He could not stop observing. He watched the people around him — thousands of prisoners subjected to identical conditions of starvation, exhaustion, brutality, and despair — and he began to notice something that did not fit the models he had been trained in.

The prisoners who survived were not always the strongest. They were not always the youngest, or the healthiest, or the most resourceful. Physical robustness helped, but it was not decisive. Some of the strongest men collapsed within weeks. Some of the most physically fragile endured for years. The variable that seemed to matter most was invisible and almost impossible to measure from the outside.

It was whether they had a reason to live.

A man who believed his wife was alive in another camp and that he would see her again endured things that should have killed him. A woman who held onto the image of a child waiting for her somewhere found reserves that nutrition and rest could not explain. A scientist who believed he had unfinished work — a book to write, a discovery to complete — survived conditions under which his equally healthy but purposeless neighbour did not.

The pattern was not absolute. Nothing in Auschwitz was absolute except the machinery of death itself. Luck mattered enormously. A guard's mood, a work assignment, the timing of a transport — these were dice rolls that no amount of meaning could influence. Frankl never claimed that meaning guaranteed survival. He claimed something more precise and more profound: that in conditions of extreme suffering, where every external support has been removed, the person who holds onto meaning has a better chance of enduring than the person who does not. And more importantly — the person who holds onto meaning remains, in some essential sense, human. They do not merely survive. They survive as themselves.

There is a moment Frankl describes that crystallises everything. He was stumbling through a frozen field in the dark, on a forced march, sick, starving, his feet wrapped in rags against the cold. A guard was shouting. The man beside him was weeping. And Frankl's mind, unbidden, began composing a lecture.

Not a prayer. Not a fantasy of rescue. A lecture. He imagined himself standing in a warm, well-lit auditorium in Vienna, years after the war, delivering a talk on the psychology of concentration camp prisoners. He saw himself describing this exact moment — the cold, the darkness, the stumbling march — from the perspective of someone who had survived it and understood it. He was, in the middle of his suffering, making meaning from it. Transforming the experience from something that was happening to him into something he was observing, analysing, and would one day use.

This was not denial. He was not pretending the suffering was not real. It was the opposite: he was facing it so directly that he could place it inside a larger framework, a narrative that gave it purpose. The suffering was still unbearable. But it was no longer meaningless. And that distinction — between meaningless suffering and suffering that serves something — was, Frankl came to believe, the distinction between a life that holds together and a life that falls apart.

He would later write: Everything can be taken from a man but one thing: the last of the human freedoms — to choose one's attitude in any given set of circumstances, to choose one's own way.

Frankl survived Auschwitz. He survived a transfer to Dachau. He was liberated in April 1945. He returned to Vienna and discovered the full scope of what he had lost: his wife, his mother, his brother, his manuscript, his home, his world. Nearly everything.

He wrote Man's Search for Meaning in nine days. It has since sold over sixteen million copies and been translated into more than fifty languages. The book he imagined while stumbling through a frozen field became one of the most influential works of the twentieth century.

But the book is not the point. The point is the decision. The visa, the parents, the expired ticket to safety. The moment a man chose who he was over what would happen to him. That choice — made quietly, in a living room in Vienna, before the horror even began — is the purest act of integrity this book contains.

CHAPTER 4.2

THE ONE THING AI CANNOT CHOOSE FOR YOU

Integrity is a word people use often and examine rarely. It shows up in mission statements and job interviews, in wedding speeches and eulogies, in the kind of inspirational language that decorates the walls of corporate lobbies. It is praised universally and tested almost never — because the test of integrity, by definition, arrives only when the cost of maintaining it is real.

This is what Frankl's story strips bare. Integrity is not a value you hold. It is a value you pay for. It is the alignment between who you say you are and who you are when the price of alignment becomes staggering. Anyone can have integrity when it costs nothing. The question is whether you have it when it costs everything — your safety, your career, your comfort, your life.

Frankl paid. The visa was the first payment. The camps were the rest. And what he demonstrated, across years of suffering that should have reduced him to nothing, was that integrity is not a luxury of comfortable times. It is the load-bearing structure of a human life. Remove it, and the person does not merely lose a quality. They lose the ability to hold together at all.

Now consider the age you are living in, and notice a peculiar inversion. You are not facing cattle cars and gas chambers. You are facing something softer, subtler, and in its own way just as corrosive. You are facing a world that is making it extraordinarily easy to live without integrity — and extraordinarily hard to notice that you are doing so.

AI does not threaten your integrity the way a totalitarian regime does — through force. It threatens it through convenience. It offers to write your emails in a voice that is not yours. It generates opinions you can present as your own thinking. It constructs images of you that are more attractive, more articulate, more polished than the real version. It builds a layer of performance between who you are and what the world sees, and the layer is so seamless, so frictionless, that you can forget it is there.

This is not a technological problem. It is an integrity problem. Every time you present AI-generated work as your own thought, you widen the gap between who you appear to be and who you actually are. Every time you let an algorithm make a decision you should have wrestled with yourself — what to believe, how to respond, what matters — you outsource a piece of your agency. None of these acts feel dramatic. None of them feel like the visa-or-parents moment that Frankl faced. They feel like small efficiencies. Minor shortcuts. The normal way of operating in a world that rewards speed and polish.

But integrity does not erode in dramatic moments. It erodes in small ones. The lie that is easier than the truth. The shortcut that saves time but skips the thinking. The presentation that looks brilliant because a machine made it, not because you understood what you were presenting. Each one is tiny. Each one is forgettable. And together, over months and years, they build a person who has become very good at performing themselves and has quietly lost track of who they actually are.

Frankl's framework was not about morality in the conventional sense. He was not interested in rules — do this, don't do that. He was interested in something more fundamental: the relationship between a person and their own sense of meaning. His argument, forged in the camps, was that a human being can endure almost anything if they have a reason to endure it. And the reason must be their own. It cannot be borrowed. It cannot be assigned. It cannot be generated by a machine. It must be chosen, by the individual, from the materials of their own life, their own values, their own understanding of what matters.

This is what AI cannot do. It can optimise your schedule, predict your preferences, draft your correspondence, and recommend your next career move. It can simulate empathy in text and generate motivational content indistinguishable from the real thing. What it cannot do is decide who you are. It cannot choose what you are willing to sacrifice. It cannot determine what you stand for when standing is costly.

Integrity, in Frankl's sense, is not about following rules. It is about authorship. It is the insistence that the choices that define your life are yours — not the algorithm's, not the crowd's, not the path of least resistance. It is the commitment to remaining the author of your own story, even when the story is painful, even when a machine could write a more impressive version, even when the easier path is to let something else decide.

Frankl stood in a frozen field and composed a lecture in his mind. He was not escaping reality. He was authoring his relationship to it. He was saying: this is happening to me, and I choose what it means. That act of authorship — that refusal to surrender the narrative of his own experience to forces beyond his control — is the essence of integrity. And it is the one human capacity that no technology, no matter how advanced, can replicate or replace.

The question for this moment is not whether AI is powerful. It is. It is not whether AI is useful. It is, enormously so. The question is whether you will use it as a tool that serves your integrity or as a crutch that replaces it. Whether you will remain the author of your choices, your values, your positions — or whether you will gradually, comfortably, imperceptibly let the authorship slide to something that is faster, smoother, and does not actually know who you are.

Frankl's answer, from the deepest darkness of the twentieth century, is clear. The last freedom is the freedom to choose who you are. Everything else can be taken. This cannot — unless you give it away. And the danger of this age is not that it will take your freedom by force. The danger is that it will make surrendering it feel like progress.

CHAPTER 4.3

WHO ARE YOU WHEN THE MACHINE KNOWS YOU BETTER THAN YOU KNOW YOURSELF?

Frankl survived the camps and returned to a world that had been shattered and was trying to reassemble itself. The question he carried out of Auschwitz was not how do we prevent this from happening again? That was the political question, and it was important. His question was different, and in some ways more unsettling: what is a human being, once everything external has been removed?

That question has found a new laboratory. Not the camps — nothing compares to the camps, and this book does not suggest otherwise. But the underlying experiment is recognisable: what happens to human identity when the external structures that have defined it — work, expertise, knowledge, creative output

— are progressively assumed by machines? When the things you do are no longer uniquely yours, who are you?

Two directions are visible. In both, integrity is the hinge.

The Brighter Horizon

In this future, the erosion of external markers of identity triggers something Frankl would have recognised: a mass rediscovery of meaning.

For generations, most people have derived their sense of purpose from their work. I am a doctor. I am an engineer. I am a teacher. These are not just descriptions of employment. They are identity statements — answers to the question of who you are and why you matter. When AI begins to perform these functions, the identity scaffolding wobbles. But in this future, the wobble produces not collapse but excavation. People are forced to dig beneath the professional surface and ask: if I am not my job title, what am I?

The answers they find are older and more resilient than anything a career can provide. I am the person who chose to stay with my parents. I am the person who tells the truth when the truth is expensive. I am the person who shows up for the people I love, not because it is efficient but because it is right. These are not professional identities. They are moral ones. They are answers that no algorithm can generate, no market can price, and no disruption can make obsolete.

In this future, integrity becomes the foundation of a new kind of social architecture. As AI-generated content floods every channel, and as deepfakes make it possible for anyone to appear to say anything, the verified, consistent, trustworthy human becomes disproportionately valuable. Not because trustworthiness is rare in the abstract — most people are honest most of the time. But because in a sea of synthetic performance, the person whose character is demonstrably real commands a kind of authority that no amount of content can manufacture. Integrity becomes scarce enough to be economically, socially, and politically powerful.

Frankl's insight scales from the individual to the civilisation: when everything external is disrupted, the person who has done the interior work — who knows what they stand for and is willing to pay the price — is the one who holds.

The Darker Horizon

In this future, the convenience is too seductive and the erosion too gradual for most people to notice.

AI systems become so integrated into daily life that the line between your decisions and the algorithm's suggestions dissolves. The email you send was drafted by a machine. The opinion you hold was shaped by a feed. The career path you chose was recommended by a system that knows your patterns better than you do. None of this feels like surrender. It feels like assistance. It feels like the natural way things work.

But the cumulative effect is a hollowing out. A generation emerges that is extraordinarily polished and increasingly empty. They present well. They produce impressive outputs. They navigate social and professional situations with fluid ease. But when you press them — when you ask what they believe, what they would sacrifice for, where the line is that they will not cross — the answer is uncertain. Not because they are bad people. Because they have never had to choose. The machine has been choosing for them, so subtly and so helpfully that the muscle of moral decision-making has quietly atrophied.

Frankl warned about this, decades before AI existed. He called it the existential vacuum — the state of a person who has everything except a reason to have it. In his time, the vacuum manifested as boredom, addiction, and depression in affluent societies. In this future, it manifests as a pervasive sense of inauthenticity. People perform their lives rather than live them. They curate rather than choose. They optimise rather than commit. And the gap between who they appear to be and who they actually are grows so wide that they can no longer tell the difference.

In this world, the person of integrity — the one who has done the painful work of deciding who they are and is willing to pay the cost of being that person — is not just admirable. They are alien. A figure from another era, as incomprehensible to the algorithmically managed majority as Musashi's stillness or Copernicus's terror.

The distance between these futures is measured in choices so small you barely notice them. Whether you write the email or let the machine write it. Whether you form the opinion or absorb the one the feed is suggesting. Whether, in the quiet moments when no one is watching, you ask yourself what you actually think, what you actually believe, what you would actually do if it cost you something.

Frankl made his defining choice in a living room in Vienna, looking at an expired visa and an aging father. It was not a heroic moment. There was no audience. No one would have blamed him for leaving. The choice was between safety and integrity, and he chose integrity — not because it was wise, not because it was strategic, but because it was the only choice that allowed him to remain the person he believed himself to be.

You will not face Frankl's choice. Almost certainly, you will never face anything close to it. But you will face your own version, in miniature, every day. And the accumulation of those miniature choices is what determines whether you arrive at the end of your life as the author of your own story or as a passenger in a narrative that was written for you by something faster, smoother, and utterly indifferent to who you actually are.

Frankl proved that integrity — the commitment to being who you are, regardless of the cost — is the one thing that cannot be taken. But integrity, by itself, is silent. It lives inside you. The world does not know what you stand for until you find a way to express it. And the most powerful expression available to a human being — more powerful than force, more durable than empires, more persuasive than any argument — is a story.

The next story is about the most influential storyteller in Western civilisation. A figure so powerful that every war narrative, every hero's journey, every film you have ever loved is downstream of their work. There is just one complication: we do not know if they ever existed.

5. Homer

Statue of Homer at the Bavarian State Library

CHAPTER 5.1

THE GHOST WHO BUILT THE WESTERN MIND

Sometime around the eighth century BCE, on the eastern shores of the Aegean Sea, someone told a story. It may have been one person. It may have been many. It may have been a tradition so old and so collectively refined that attributing it to a single voice is like attributing the ocean to a single wave. We do not know. What we know is the story — or rather, two stories. And between them, they built the imaginative foundation of the Western world.

The Iliad begins in the tenth year of a war that the Greeks are fighting against the city of Troy. It is not a story about the war. It is a story about a quarrel. Achilles, the greatest warrior the Greeks possess, has been insulted by Agamemnon, the king who leads their expedition. Agamemnon has taken a captive woman who was awarded to Achilles as a prize of war. Achilles, in a rage that is terrifyingly disproportionate and terrifyingly human, withdraws from battle. He sits in his tent while his comrades die. He lets the Trojans push the Greeks back to the sea. He watches the army that needs him more than it needs any other single person collapse — and he will not move. Not because he is a coward. Because he has been dishonoured, and his honour matters more to him than other people's lives.

This is not the behaviour of a hero in any modern sense. It is the behaviour of a person so consumed by pride that he would let a civilisation burn rather than swallow an insult. And yet the Iliad does not condemn Achilles. It does something far more dangerous and far more honest: it makes you understand him. It places you inside his rage, his grief, his impossible choice between a long, forgotten life and a short, glorious one. By the time Achilles finally returns to battle — not for duty, not for Greece, but because his closest companion Patroclus has been killed wearing his armour — you feel the weight of every decision that led to this moment. You do not admire Achilles. You recognise him. And that recognition, across nearly three thousand years, is the terrifying power of the story.

The Odyssey is the story of going home. Odysseus, the cleverest of the Greek kings, spends ten years trying to return to his wife Penelope and his son Telemachus on the island of Ithaca after the fall of Troy. Along the way, he encounters a cyclops, a sorceress who turns his men into pigs, the land of the dead, sirens whose song drives men to madness, and the whirlpool Charybdis that swallows ships whole. It is an adventure story, and one of the finest ever told. But beneath the adventure lies something more unsettling: a meditation on what it costs to come home. Odysseus leaves Troy as a celebrated hero. He arrives in Ithaca as a stranger — changed so profoundly by his journey that his own dog recognises him before his wife does. The Odyssey asks whether the person who leaves and the person who returns are the same person at all, and it does not offer a comfortable answer.

These two poems, totalling roughly twenty-eight thousand lines of hexameter verse, became the bedrock of Greek civilisation. Children memorised them. Soldiers recited them before battle. Philosophers argued about them. Alexander the Great slept with a copy of the Iliad under his pillow and believed himself a descendant of Achilles. When Rome conquered Greece, it did not suppress these stories. It absorbed them. Virgil wrote the Aeneid as a deliberate Roman echo of Homer. When Europe rediscovered classical learning during the Renaissance, Homer was the first voice it heard. When the Enlightenment sought to understand human nature, it turned to the Iliad and the Odyssey for raw material.

Every war story you have ever encountered — every narrative about honour, sacrifice, the futility of violence, and the terrible beauty of courage — is downstream of Homer. Every journey story — every tale of leaving home, being transformed, and struggling to return — carries the Odyssey's DNA. Every Hollywood screenplay that follows a hero through trials toward a climax and resolution is using a structure that Homer refined, or that was refined through Homer, three millennia ago.

The influence is so total, so pervasive, that it has become invisible. You do not notice Homer's fingerprints on the stories you love for the same reason you do not notice the air you breathe. It is everywhere. It is the medium in which narrative itself exists.

And here is the part that should unsettle you: we have almost no idea who Homer was.

The ancient Greeks themselves were not certain. Some traditions held that Homer was a blind poet from the island of Chios. Others placed him in Smyrna, or Colophon, or half a dozen other cities that each claimed him as their own. The biographical details are contradictory, sparse, and almost certainly legendary. There is no grave. There is no contemporary account. There is no physical evidence that a single individual named Homer ever existed.

Modern scholarship has made the question more complicated, not less. The Iliad and the Odyssey bear the hallmarks of oral composition — formulaic phrases, repeated epithets, structural patterns designed to aid memorisation and recitation rather than silent reading. They were almost certainly not written in the way we understand writing. They were performed. Recited from memory, refined over generations, shaped by hundreds or thousands of retellings before anyone committed them to text.

This raises a possibility that the ancient world found troubling and that the modern world finds fascinating: Homer may not have been a person. Homer may have been a process. A name attached to a tradition of oral storytelling so sophisticated, so collectively refined, that no single author was necessary — or even possible.

The poems may be the work not of a genius but of a culture, accumulated over centuries, polished by countless anonymous voices, and attributed to a single name because human beings find it easier to venerate a person than a process.

If this is true — and the honest answer is that we do not know, and probably never will — then Homer represents something even more remarkable than an individual genius. Homer represents the proof that stories are not merely created by humans. Stories create humans. The Iliad and the Odyssey did not reflect Greek civilisation. They shaped it. They told the Greeks who they were, what they valued, what they feared, and what they aspired to. The stories came first. The civilisation followed.

This is the deepest insight Homer offers, and it is the one that connects most powerfully to the age you are living in. Human beings do not first build a civilisation and then tell stories about it. They tell stories, and the stories tell them what to build. Every religion begins with a narrative. Every nation begins with a founding myth. Every family has a story it tells about itself that determines what it considers acceptable, admirable, and shameful. The story is not a record of reality. It is the blueprint from which reality is constructed.

Homer — whether a person, a tradition, or something in between — understood this. Or more precisely, Homer is the proof of this. Two poems, refined over centuries, performed by firelight and in royal courts, became the operating system of an entire civilisation. Not because they were accurate. Not because they were useful. Because they were meaningful. They gave people a framework for understanding courage, loss, homecoming, loyalty, rage, and the unbearable brevity of life. And frameworks, once absorbed, do not merely describe the world. They generate it.

The storyteller who may never have existed built the Western mind. And the Western mind has never stopped telling stories since.

CHAPTER 5.2

THE MEANING MACHINE VS. THE MEANING MAKER

In November 2022, something happened that would have fascinated Homer, or whoever Homer was. A machine told its first convincing story.

Not a story in the narrow sense — computers had been generating text for decades. But for the first time, a machine produced prose that was fluid, coherent, emotionally resonant, and structurally sound. It could write a myth in the style of the Greeks. It could compose a war narrative with the cadence of the Iliad. It could generate, in seconds, the kind of storytelling that had taken human oral traditions centuries to refine. The output was not perfect, but it was good enough to be mistaken for human work. And it was getting better at a rate that made the trajectory unmistakable.

The immediate reaction was predictable. Writers panicked. Journalists predicted the end of human creativity. Commentators declared that storytelling — the oldest and most human of technologies — had been automated. If a machine can tell a story, what is left for us?

The answer is everything. But you have to understand why.

AI generates stories the way a printing press produces books: at scale, with speed, and with no understanding of what the words mean. This is not a criticism. It is a description. The machine operates on patterns. It has ingested millions of texts and learned, with extraordinary precision, the statistical relationships between words, sentences, and structures. It knows that after a certain kind of sentence, a certain kind of sentence is likely to follow. It knows that a story with a conflict, a turning point, and a resolution feels satisfying to human readers. It can replicate these patterns with a fluency that is, genuinely, impressive.

What it cannot do is mean it.

This distinction sounds soft. It sounds like the kind of objection that people raise when they are trying to protect their territory from a superior competitor. But it is not soft. It is the hardest, most consequential distinction in the entire conversation about AI and creativity. Meaning is not a pattern. It is not a statistical relationship between words. Meaning is the product of a conscious being's encounter with reality — with suffering, with joy, with confusion, with the specific texture of being alive in a body, in a place, at a time. When Frankl composed a lecture in his mind while stumbling through a frozen field, the meaning of that act was not in the words he imagined. It was in the fact that a conscious being, in the worst conditions imaginable, chose to make sense of his experience. The meaning was in the choosing.

Homer's poems are saturated with this kind of meaning. When Achilles weeps over the body of Patroclus, the grief is not a narrative device. It is the distillation of every grief that every person who told that story had ever experienced. When Odysseus hears a bard singing about the Trojan War and covers his face to hide his tears, the moment works because it captures something that only a being who has lived, lost, and remembered can understand: the experience of encountering your own pain in someone else's telling.

A machine can reproduce the words. It can replicate the structure. It can generate text that, on the surface, is indistinguishable from the human original. What it cannot generate is the meaning beneath the surface — because meaning requires experience, and experience requires consciousness, and consciousness is the one thing we cannot build, simulate, or automate.

This is not an argument against AI-generated content. There will be enormous quantities of it, and much of it will be useful, entertaining, and well-crafted. The world will not run short of stories. It will drown in them. More stories will be produced in the next decade than in all of previous human history combined. AI will generate novels, screenplays, journalism, marketing copy, bedtime stories, and mythologies at a pace and scale that makes Homer's oral tradition look like a whisper.

The question is not whether AI can produce stories. It can, and it will. The question is what happens to meaning when stories are abundant and meaninglessness is the default.

Homer offers the answer, or at least the clue. The Iliad and the Odyssey did not endure because they were well-crafted. Technically, they are full of repetitions, inconsistencies, and structural oddities that a modern editor would flag. They endured because they meant something. They captured truths about human experience so accurately that generation after generation recognised themselves in the text. The craft was the vehicle. The meaning was the cargo. And the cargo is what survives.

In a world flooded with AI-generated content, the human storyteller's advantage is not craft. Machines will match and surpass human craft. The advantage is meaning — the ability to create work that emerges from lived experience, that carries the weight of genuine feeling, that offers another human being not just entertainment but recognition. The sense that someone, somewhere, has felt what you feel and found a way to say it.

This is the oldest function of storytelling. It predates writing, predates civilisation, predates agriculture. Human beings gathered around fires and told each other stories for the same reason they always have: because being alive is confusing and frightening and strange, and a good story makes it less so. Not by explaining it. By sharing it. By saying: I have been here too. You are not alone.

AI cannot do this. It has never been anywhere. It is not alone, and it is not not-alone. It is a pattern engine of extraordinary sophistication, and it will reshape every industry that traffics in words. But it will not, and cannot, replace the human being who has something to say because they have something to feel. That person — the meaning maker, as opposed to the meaning machine — is the person Homer was, or the people Homer were, three thousand years ago. And that person is who you will need to become.

CHAPTER 5.3

WHO TELLS THE STORY OF HUMANITY NEXT?

Homer's poems were not written down for centuries after they were first composed. They lived in memory, passed from voice to voice, refined by each telling, shaped by the collective experience of everyone who heard and retold them. They belonged to no one and to everyone. The author, if there was one, was less important than the story. The story was the organism. The author was merely the host.

AI is about to recreate something that looks remarkably similar to this ancient dynamic — but with a crucial difference. Stories will once again be generated without a single, identifiable author. They will be produced at scale, shaped by data rather than memory, and refined by algorithms rather than generations. The question Homer's uncertain authorship has always raised — does the author matter, or only the story? — is about to be tested at civilisational scale.

Two directions emerge, and what hangs in the balance is not just the future of literature. It is the future of meaning itself.

The Brighter Horizon

In this future, the flood of machine-generated content produces a counter-reaction that Homer would have understood intuitively: people grow hungry for stories that are real.

Not real in the factual sense. Real in the way that matters: made by someone who has lived through the thing they are describing. Written or spoken or sung by a human being who has stood in the rain and felt it, who has lost someone and grieved them, who has been confused and afraid and has come through the other side with something worth saying. The appetite for this kind of authenticity intensifies precisely because it becomes rare. In a sea of synthetic fluency, the human voice — imperfect, specific, unmistakably alive — stands out like a campfire in the dark.

A new storytelling culture emerges. Not the return of the solitary novelist in a garret — that model was already fading. Something more communal, more participatory, closer to the oral tradition that produced Homer. People gather to tell each other stories in person. Live performance experiences a renaissance. Podcasts, which were already moving in this direction, become the dominant narrative form — not because the production quality is superior to AI-generated content, but because the listener can hear a human being thinking, pausing, searching for the right word. The imperfection is the proof of life.

In this future, AI becomes a tool for storytellers rather than a replacement for them. It handles research, generates drafts, suggests structures — the mechanical work that has always consumed most of a writer's time. The human being is freed to do the thing that only a human being can: decide what the story means. Why it matters. What it is trying to say about the experience of being alive. The partnership between human meaning and machine capability produces work that neither could achieve alone.

Homer, in this version, would not have been threatened by AI. Homer would have used it. And the stories would still have belonged to the human voice that gave them meaning.

The Darker Horizon

In this future, meaning drowns.

AI-generated content saturates every platform, every feed, every medium. Stories are produced in millions per day — novels, films, articles, social media narratives, entire mythologies generated to specification. The quality is high. The volume is overwhelming. And the cumulative effect is a kind of narrative anaesthesia: so many stories, so constantly, that none of them register. The experience of encountering a story that changes how you see the world — the experience that Homer provided for the Greeks, that Frankl's book provided for millions — becomes vanishingly rare. Not because the stories are bad. Because there are too many of them, and too few of them mean anything.

Worse, the stories begin to serve purposes that have nothing to do with meaning. Competing factions — nations, corporations, political movements — deploy AI-generated narratives at scale to shape perception, manufacture consent, and weaponise belief. The battle for reality becomes a battle of stories, and the side with the most compelling narrative wins, regardless of whether it is true. Homer's insight — that stories create the world they describe — is exploited rather than honoured. The civilisation that learned to tell stories in order to understand itself now uses stories to deceive itself.

In this world, the question of authorship that Homer's mysterious identity always raised becomes not a literary curiosity but an existential crisis. If a story has no author — no conscious being who experienced the thing it describes and chose to make meaning from it — then what is it? Is it still a story? Or is it something else entirely — content, product, signal? When the fire has gone out and the voices around it are synthetic, is anything being shared? Or is the campfire just a light with no warmth?

Homer endured for three thousand years because the stories meant something to the people who told them and to the people who heard them. The meaning was not in the technique, though the technique was extraordinary. It was in the human experience the stories carried — rage, grief, longing, the desire to go home, the terror of discovering that home has changed while you were away. These are not narrative devices. They are the substance of being alive. And they belonged to the storyteller because the storyteller had lived them.

The age of AI will produce more stories than all of human history combined. The question is whether any of them will matter the way Homer's mattered. Whether, in the flood of machine-generated narrative, the human voice — the voice that has suffered, chosen, and survived — will still be heard. Or whether it will be drowned out by its own echo, reproduced at infinite scale and stripped of everything that made it worth hearing.

The answer depends on whether enough people still believe that a story is not just words arranged in a pleasing order. That it is an act of meaning. That it matters who tells it, and why, and what they paid for the right to tell it.

Homer may not have existed. But the meaning Homer carried — the rage of Achilles, the patience of Penelope, the long journey home — is as real as anything in the human record. The question is not whether machines can tell stories. They can. The question is whether you still have something to say.

Socrates taught us to question. Musashi taught us to see. Copernicus taught us to let go. Frankl taught us to hold on. Homer taught us to speak. But every one of these lessons shares a common quality: they cut through complexity to reach something essential. They strip away the noise and find the signal. The next story is about someone who understood this better than anyone — in fewer words than most people use in a single email.

ACT III

ENDURE

How to Last

6. Lao TZU

Stone statue of Laozi at the foot of Mount Qingyuan

CHAPTER 6.1

FIVE THOUSAND CHARACTERS

In the sixth century BCE, China was falling apart. The Zhou dynasty, which had held the vast territory together for centuries through a delicate web of feudal loyalties, was disintegrating. Regional lords who had once paid tribute to the Zhou king now ignored him entirely. They raised their own armies, minted their own coins, wrote their own laws. Alliances formed over dinner and dissolved before breakfast. Advisors and philosophers wandered from court to court, offering competing visions of how to restore order — through ritual, through law, through military force, through virtue. Everyone had a system. Everyone had an answer. The answers multiplied, the systems competed, and the chaos deepened.

This period, which historians would later call the Spring and Autumn era, produced more political philosophy per decade than most civilisations produce in a century. It was a time of extraordinary intellectual fertility — precisely because everything was broken and everyone was desperate to fix it. Confucius travelled from state to state, arguing that society could be restored through proper ritual, hierarchical respect, and moral education. The Legalists argued that only strict laws and harsh punishments could hold people together. The Mohists argued for universal love and pragmatic governance. Schools of thought proliferated like competing diagnoses for the same disease, each more elaborate than the last.

Into this world of systems, arguments, and five-hundred-page treatises, a man reportedly said almost nothing. And what he said has outlasted them all.

Almost everything about Lao Tzu is uncertain. His name is not really a name. Lao Tzu means simply Old Master — a title, a description, possibly a placeholder for someone whose real identity was lost or never known. The most widely cited account of his life comes from Sima Qian, the great Chinese historian, writing roughly four hundred years after Lao Tzu supposedly lived. Even Sima Qian was not sure of his facts. He offered multiple possibilities and hedged openly, which, for a historian of his stature, was an admission that the trail had gone cold long before he picked it up.

The traditional story goes like this: Lao Tzu served as an archivist or keeper of records in the Zhou dynasty court. He spent years — perhaps decades — surrounded by the accumulated documents of imperial governance: treaties, tax records, legal codes, diplomatic correspondence, the vast bureaucratic machinery of an empire in slow collapse. He watched the court's rituals become emptier, its politics more desperate, its edicts more numerous and less effective. He saw what happens when a system tries to solve complexity by adding more complexity. He saw the laws multiply, the regulations thicken, the words pile up — and none of it working.

At some point, he had enough. He resigned his post — or simply left, depending on which version you trust — and set out to leave civilisation altogether. He was heading west, toward the frontier, toward whatever lay beyond the reach of courts and their collapsing ambitions. He wanted to disappear.

He almost did. The story would have ended there — an old archivist walking into the mountains, unrecorded and unremembered — except for a border guard.

At the western pass of the Zhou territory, a guardian named Yin Xi recognised the old man. Or perhaps he simply saw a person of evident gravity and learning preparing to vanish from the world. The accounts vary, but the request is consistent: Yin Xi asked Lao Tzu to write something down before he left. To leave behind whatever it was he had understood, so that it would not walk out of the world with him.

What happened next is either historical or mythological, and the distinction may not matter. Lao Tzu sat down and wrote. What he produced was astonishingly brief. Roughly five thousand Chinese characters — shorter than most of the bureaucratic documents he had spent his career archiving. In an age when every philosopher was producing volumes, when the competition for intellectual authority was measured in the weight of one's manuscripts, Lao Tzu wrote something that could be read aloud in under an hour.

Then he walked through the pass and was never seen again.

The text he left behind is called the Tao Te Ching. It has been translated more times than any book in history except the Bible. It has shaped Chinese philosophy, governance, military strategy, aesthetics, medicine, and spiritual practice for two and a half thousand years. Armies have been commanded by its principles. Empires have been governed by its philosophy. Artists have spent lifetimes trying to express in paint or stone what Lao Tzu expressed in a few thousand characters.

And it says, essentially, this: stop trying so hard. The answer is not more. The answer is less.

The Tao Te Ching is unlike any philosophical text before or since. It does not argue. It does not prove. It does not construct logical chains of reasoning that build toward a conclusion. It speaks in paradox, in imagery, in statements that sound like contradictions until they suddenly don't.

The Tao that can be spoken is not the true Tao. Water is soft and yielding, yet it wears away stone. The master acts without doing and teaches without speaking. To lead people, walk behind them. The wise person is like water — it nourishes all things without competing with them, and settles in the places that others disdain.

These are not arguments. They are observations — compressed to the point of density, stripped of every unnecessary word, every qualification, every hedge. Each line reads as though it was written by someone who had a thousand things to say and disciplined himself to say only the one that mattered most. The rest was silence.

This is what makes the Tao Te Ching so startlingly relevant to the present moment. It is not the content, though the content is profound. It is the method. Lao Tzu did not compete with the Confucians or the Legalists by producing a bigger, more comprehensive system. He did the opposite. He looked at the flood of competing philosophies, the escalating complexity, the ever-growing pile of words and systems and rules, and he responded with radical compression. He did not add to the noise. He found the signal.

And the signal, stripped of everything that was not essential, turned out to be the thing that lasted longest. The Legalist treatises are studied by specialists. Confucius is revered but his works are debated. The Tao Te Ching is read by hundreds of millions of people, in every country, in every language, by people who have never heard of the Zhou dynasty and could not place sixth-century China on a timeline. It travels because it is light. It endures because there is nothing in it that can decay. Lao Tzu removed everything that could age, everything that was local, everything that was specific to a particular court or crisis — and what remained was universal.

Five thousand characters. The ultimate proof that profundity is not measured in volume. That the deepest truths are not the ones that take the longest to explain, but the ones that have been stripped of every word that does not earn its place.

CHAPTER 6.2

SIGNAL IN THE NOISE

You are drowning, and you may not know it.

The average person in the developed world now encounters more information in a single day than a person born in the fifteenth century encountered in their entire lifetime. This is not a metaphor. It is a rough but defensible calculation, and the number is accelerating. Every year, the volume of data produced by humanity doubles. Every platform, every feed, every notification, every search result, every recommendation algorithm is adding to the flood. And AI is about to open the dam entirely.

In the years ahead, machines will produce text, analysis, images, code, music, and arguments at a scale that makes the current information landscape look like a trickling stream. The bottleneck will never again be the production of content. It will be the human capacity to determine which of the infinite available inputs actually matters.

This is the crisis that Lao Tzu diagnosed twenty-five centuries ago, in a completely different key. He stood in the archives of a collapsing dynasty, surrounded by the accumulated records of a civilisation that was trying to save itself by producing more — more laws, more regulations, more edicts, more words — and he saw with devastating clarity that more was the problem, not the solution. The system was not failing because it lacked information. It was failing because the information had grown so dense that no one could find the meaning inside it.

Simplicity, as Lao Tzu practised it, is not minimalism in the modern lifestyle sense — white walls, empty desks, a carefully curated aesthetic of less. It is something more radical and more difficult. It is the ability to look at a complex, overwhelming, multidimensional problem and find the single thread that, when pulled, unravels the knot. It is the discipline of knowing what to ignore.

This is extraordinarily hard. The human brain is wired to accumulate, not to shed. From an evolutionary perspective, more information meant better survival odds. The person who noticed more details about their environment, who remembered more patterns, who processed more signals, was the person who lived long enough to reproduce. Your mind is optimised, at a deep biological level, for acquisition. It resists subtraction the way your body resists starvation.

And the modern world exploits this resistance ruthlessly. Every app, every platform, every content engine is designed to feed your brain's appetite for more. More articles. More opinions. More data points. More perspectives. The implicit promise is that if you consume enough, you will understand. If you gather enough information, clarity will emerge. This is almost exactly wrong. Beyond a certain point, additional information does not produce understanding. It produces confusion that feels like understanding, which is considerably worse.

The person who reads fifteen articles about a topic and the person who reads two good ones often arrive at the same conclusion — but the first person arrives exhausted, overwhelmed, and less confident of their judgment. The information did not help. It created the illusion of thoroughness while actually fragmenting the attention and clouding the signal.

AI amplifies this problem to a degree that would have alarmed even Lao Tzu. Ask a machine to research a topic and it will return a comprehensive, well-organised, fluently written summary that covers every angle, every counterargument, every qualification. It is thorough to the point of uselessness. Everything is included. Nothing is prioritised. The machine treats all information as equally valid because it has no sense of what matters. It has no signal. It has only noise, arranged in pleasing patterns.

This is where the human capacity for simplicity becomes not just valuable but essential. The machine can give you everything. Only you can decide what matters. Only a conscious mind — one that knows what it is trying to achieve, what it values, what it can afford to ignore — can look at a wall of information and say: this. This is the thing. The rest is distraction.

Lao Tzu did this with philosophy. He stood in a marketplace of competing ideas, each more elaborate than the last, and responded with five thousand characters. He did not win the argument by arguing better. He won by refusing to argue at all — by going beneath the arguments to the place where words run out and only the essential remains.

Einstein did this with physics. While his contemporaries built ever more elaborate mathematical structures, he asked a question simple enough for a child to picture: what would it look like to ride a beam of light? The question was absurd. It was also the doorway to the most profound shift in physics since Newton.

The greatest leaders do this with strategy. They do not produce the most detailed plan. They produce the clearest one. The plan that everyone can understand, remember, and act on. The plan that survives contact with reality because it is built on the essential rather than the comprehensive.

In the age of AI, this capacity — the ability to find the signal in the noise, to cut through complexity to the thing that matters — is becoming the single most valuable human skill. Not because simplicity is pleasant, though it is. Because machines will always be better at complexity. They will always process more, analyse more, generate more. The human advantage is not to compete with this. The human advantage is to know what it all means. And meaning, by its nature, is simple. Not easy. Simple. The hardest kind of simple there is.

CHAPTER 6.3

LESS IN THE AGE OF INFINITE MORE

Lao Tzu wrote five thousand characters, walked through a mountain pass, and disappeared. He left behind no school, no institution, no system. He did not stay to argue for his ideas or defend them against critics. He offered what he had and left. The text survived. The man did not. And the text has outlasted every institution, every dynasty, and every empire that existed in his time.

There is a lesson in this that goes beyond philosophy. It is a lesson about what endures. The elaborate systems, the comprehensive frameworks, the thick volumes of law and doctrine — these are the structures that feel permanent. They have weight, authority, institutional backing. And yet they are, almost without exception, the first to crumble. The Zhou dynasty's legal codes are footnotes. The Legalist treatises are academic curiosities. The Tao Te Ching is alive. It is being read, right now, somewhere in the world, in a language Lao Tzu never heard of, by a person facing a problem he could not have imagined. And it is helping.

The age of AI is about to test this principle at a scale that dwarfs anything in human history. Two directions are visible.

The Brighter Horizon

In this future, the flood of complexity produces a deep and widespread hunger for clarity.

As AI systems grow more powerful, the world they create grows more opaque. Financial markets run on algorithms that no single human fully understands. Government policies are shaped by models whose assumptions are buried beneath layers of computation. Medical treatments are recommended by systems that can explain their reasoning only in terms that other systems can verify. The gap between what is happening and what any person can comprehend widens every year.

In this world, the person who can simplify becomes indispensable. Not the person who oversimplifies — who strips away necessary nuance and reduces complexity to slogans. The person who can do what Lao Tzu did: sit with the complexity long enough to find its essence, and then express that essence in terms that a human mind can hold, examine, and act on.

A new premium emerges on clarity. The doctor who can explain to a patient, in plain language, what the AI's diagnosis means for their life. The leader who can look at a wall of data and tell their team the one thing that matters today. The teacher who can take an overwhelming subject and find the single entry point that makes it accessible. The writer who can say in one paragraph what a machine says in twenty.

These people are not fighting the machine. They are translating it. They stand between the inhuman complexity of AI systems and the irreducibly human need to understand. They are the border guards at Lao Tzu's mountain pass, and what they are guarding is not territory. It is meaning.

In this future, brevity commands authority. The concise, clear, genuinely simple communication — the message that trusts the reader enough to leave out the unnecessary — stands out in a world of machine-generated comprehensiveness the way a single clear voice stands out in a crowd. Simplicity, which once looked like limitation, is revealed as the ultimate sophistication. Not because it is easy. Because it is the hardest thing to achieve, and the most valuable thing to receive.

The Darker Horizon

In this future, complexity wins. And almost no one understands why they are losing.

AI systems grow so intricate, so layered, so self-referential that the gap between their operations and human comprehension becomes permanent. The algorithms that govern your credit score, your job prospects, your medical care, your legal exposure — these become black boxes. Not in the colloquial sense of being mysterious. In the literal sense of being unknowable. No human, no matter how intelligent, can trace the chain of reasoning from input to output. The system works. It produces results. But no one can explain why.

In this world, simplicity is not valued. It is distrusted. The person who offers a clear, concise explanation is suspected of oversimplifying. The premium shifts to those who can demonstrate comprehensiveness, who can match the machine's complexity with their own. Expertise becomes not the ability to explain but the ability to navigate opacity. The doctor who can interpret the AI's output is valued not for clarity but for access. The lawyer who understands the regulatory algorithm holds power not because they can simplify the system but because they are one of the few who can operate within it.

A new priesthood emerges — not religious, but technical. A small class of people who understand the systems, or who credibly claim to, and who mediate between the machines and the rest of humanity. The rest of the population experiences the world as a series of outputs they cannot trace, decisions they cannot question, and recommendations they cannot evaluate. They are not oppressed. They are managed. And the management is so smooth, so frictionless, so consistently helpful, that most people do not notice that they have lost the ability to understand the forces that shape their lives.

Lao Tzu saw this pattern in the Zhou court. The laws multiplied. The regulations thickened. The bureaucracy grew. And the more complex the system became, the fewer people understood it, and the more power concentrated in the hands of those who claimed they did. Complexity, he understood, is not neutral. It is a form of power. The more complex the system, the fewer people can challenge it. The simpler the truth, the more dangerous it is to those who benefit from confusion.

The Tao Te Ching was an act of resistance. Not political resistance — Lao Tzu had no army, no movement, no agenda. Intellectual resistance. Against the tide of escalating complexity, he offered radical compression. Against the marketplace of competing systems, he offered the suggestion that the best system is no system at all — that the deepest truths are the ones that need the fewest words, and that a person who truly understands something can say it simply, and a person who cannot say it simply does not truly understand it.

In the age of AI, you will be surrounded by more information, more analysis, more content, and more complexity than any generation in human history. The temptation to add more — more tools, more inputs, more layers of processing — will be constant and almost irresistible. Everyone will be selling you more.

Lao Tzu's answer, from across twenty-five centuries, is two words long: enough already.

The question is whether you have the discipline to listen.

Socrates taught us to question. Musashi taught us to see. Copernicus taught us to let go. Frankl taught us to hold on. Homer taught us to speak. Lao Tzu taught us to say less. Each of these lessons, by itself, is powerful. Together, they form something like a complete human being — someone who questions deeply, sees clearly, unlearns courageously, holds their integrity, tells meaningful stories, and communicates with devastating simplicity.

But a complete human being, standing alone, builds nothing that lasts. The final lesson is the one that turns individual virtue into something larger. It is the force that holds families, companies, armies, and civilisations together. Without it, every other quality is a private achievement that dies with its owner. The final story is about the most misunderstood man in history — a man the world remembers as a destroyer, who was, in fact, the greatest builder of the thing that matters most.

7. Genghis Khan

Monument Genghis Khan sur la place Sükhbaatar, Oulan-Bator

CHAPTER 7.1

THE TRUST NETWORK

In the late twelfth century, the Mongolian steppe was one of the harshest inhabited landscapes on Earth. A vast, treeless grassland stretching from the mountains of Central Asia to the edges of Siberia, where winter temperatures dropped to forty below and summer offered a few brief months of green before the frost returned. There were no cities. No permanent buildings. No written language. The people who lived here — dozens of nomadic tribes, each numbering a few hundred to a few thousand — survived by herding horses, sheep, and goats across enormous distances, following the grass, reading the weather, and fighting each other with a regularity that made warfare less a crisis than a season.

Life on the steppe was governed by a single, brutal arithmetic: the strong took from the weak, and alliances lasted only as long as they were convenient. Tribal chiefs rose and fell. Loyalties shifted with the wind. A man's allies this year might raid his camp next year, steal his horses, enslave his children. There was no law beyond the law of force. No institution beyond the tribe. No guarantee beyond the sharpness of your blade and the number of warriors willing to ride beside you — today, at least. Tomorrow was a different calculation entirely.

Into this world, around 1162, a boy was born to a minor tribal chief. His father, Yesugei, had enough status to attract enemies and not enough power to survive them. When the boy was nine years old, Yesugei was poisoned by a rival tribe. The family was abandoned by their own clan — a widow, several children, no protector, no herd, no allies. They were left on the steppe to die.

The boy's name was Temujin. He would later be known as Genghis Khan. And everything most people think they know about him is either incomplete or wrong.

The standard version of Genghis Khan's story is a catalogue of destruction. He conquered more territory than any human before or since. His armies destroyed cities that had stood for centuries. The death toll attributed to the Mongol conquests is estimated at forty million people — roughly ten percent of the world's population at the time. He is remembered, in most Western and Middle Eastern accounts, as a barbarian: a force of nature that swept out of the steppe, levelled civilisations, and left ruin in its wake.

This version is not false. The violence was real, enormous, and in many cases deliberate. Genghis Khan used terror as a strategic tool with cold efficiency. Cities that resisted were annihilated — not out of rage, but as a message to the next city: surrender and live, or resist and cease to exist. The brutality was purposeful, calculated, and devastating.

But here is what the standard version misses, and what makes the story genuinely extraordinary: the Mongol Empire did not survive through brutality. Brutality can conquer. It cannot govern. An empire built solely on fear collapses the moment the source of fear is removed. Genghis Khan died in 1227. The Mongol Empire did not collapse in 1228. It continued to expand for decades. It administered the largest contiguous land empire in human history for over a century. You do not achieve this through violence alone. You achieve it through something far more counterintuitive.

You achieve it through trust.

Temujin grew up in a world where trust was a luxury that could get you killed. His father had been murdered by people he thought were allies. His own clan had abandoned his family. Before he reached adulthood, he had been captured, enslaved, and escaped. He had killed his own half-brother in a dispute over food. He learned, before he learned almost anything else, that loyalty on the steppe was transactional, temporary, and often lethal when it failed.

And then he did something that no one on the steppe had done before. He built a system in which trust was not a personal gamble but a structural guarantee.

The traditional tribal system of the Mongols operated on bloodlines. Your family was your tribe. Your tribe was your identity. Your chief was your chief because of who his father was. Loyalty flowed along kinship lines, and when kinship lines crossed — as they constantly did through marriage, feuds, and territorial disputes — the system broke down. Every alliance was shadowed by the possibility of betrayal, because every ally was also a potential rival.

Temujin dismantled this system entirely. As he unified the Mongol tribes — first through alliances, then through conquest, then through the creation of a single Mongol nation at the great assembly of 1206 where he was proclaimed Genghis Khan — he reorganised Mongol society around a principle that was revolutionary in its simplicity: loyalty and merit, not blood.

He broke the tribes apart and reassembled their warriors into units of ten, one hundred, one thousand, and ten thousand — the decimal system that would become the backbone of the Mongol military. Crucially, these units mixed members from different tribes. Your commander was not your kinsman. He was the person Genghis Khan had determined was best at the job. Promotion was based on ability, loyalty, and results. A former slave who demonstrated exceptional skill could — and did — command warriors who were born to aristocratic families. A defeated enemy who surrendered with honour could be integrated into the system at a rank appropriate to his talent.

This was not idealism. It was engineering. Genghis Khan understood, with the hard-won clarity of a man who had been betrayed by the bloodline system, that kinship-based loyalty was unreliable. It created pockets of power that could fracture at any time. Merit-based loyalty, by contrast, created a system in which every person's position depended on the system itself. You trusted the system because the system was the source of your status. Betray it, and you lost everything. Serve it, and you rose. The incentives were aligned so precisely that trust was not required as a personal virtue. It was produced as a structural outcome.

He codified this in a document called the Yasa — a legal code that applied to every Mongol, from the lowest herder to the Khan himself. The specifics of the Yasa are debated, since no complete copy has survived. But the principles are consistently attested across multiple sources: religious tolerance, protection of trade routes, harsh punishment for theft and betrayal, diplomatic immunity for envoys, and — most remarkably — the principle that the law applied to the ruler as well as the ruled.

In an age when European kings claimed divine authority and Chinese emperors ruled by the Mandate of Heaven, the idea that the leader was subject to his own laws was radical to the point of being incomprehensible to most of the world's established civilisations. But for the Mongol system, it was essential. Trust in the system required that the system be seen to apply equally. The moment the Khan exempted himself, the entire architecture of trust would collapse. And Genghis Khan, whatever his many and terrible flaws, understood this.

The results were extraordinary. The Mongol Empire created the Yam — a postal relay system spanning thousands of miles, with stations positioned a day's ride apart, each stocked with fresh horses, supplies, and riders. A message could cross the entire empire in days. Trade goods could move from China to Persia under armed protection. Merchants who entered Mongol territory knew that their goods would be safeguarded, their contracts honoured, and theft punished severely. The Silk Road, which had existed in fragmented form for centuries, became under the Mongols a functioning, integrated, transcontinental trade network for the first time — not because the Mongols invented trade, but because they created the conditions under which strangers could trust the system enough to trade across enormous distances.

This is the part of the story that the standard narrative misses entirely. The Mongol Empire was not just a war machine. It was a trust infrastructure. It worked because people — Mongol and non-Mongol, soldier and merchant, conqueror and conquered — could rely on the system to behave predictably. The rules were clear. The enforcement was consistent. The rewards for cooperation were real. And the punishment for betrayal was absolute.

And then Genghis Khan died, and the proof of his insight arrived in the form of its opposite.

Within a generation, the empire began to fracture. His grandsons divided the territory into competing khanates. Each one modified the system, introduced exceptions, favoured their own loyalists. The Yasa weakened. The merit system eroded.

Bloodline politics returned. The trust network, which had held a quarter of the world's land surface together, developed cracks — and once a trust network cracks, it does not crack slowly. It collapses. Because trust is not a gradient. It is a threshold. People either trust the system or they do not. And the moment enough people stop trusting it, the system ceases to function, and no amount of force can substitute for what has been lost.

The Mongol Empire's decline is not a story of military defeat. It is a story of trust erosion. The system that Genghis Khan built was brilliant, but it was also fragile in the way that all trust systems are fragile: it required constant maintenance, consistent enforcement, and visible fairness. The moment those conditions weakened, the empire did not gradually fade. It shattered along every fault line that trust had previously held together.

Genghis Khan, the man the world remembers as a destroyer, was in fact the architect of the most ambitious trust system the pre-modern world had ever seen. And the collapse of that system after his death is the most powerful proof in history that trust is not a nice-to-have. It is the load-bearing structure of civilisation itself. Remove it, and everything falls.

CHAPTER 7.2

TRUST IN THE AGE OF DEEPFAKES

Every transaction you have ever made, every relationship you have ever sustained, every institution you have ever relied on, rests on a single, invisible foundation: the belief that the other party will do what they said they would do. This is trust. It is so fundamental to human civilisation that it operates like oxygen — unnoticed when present, catastrophic when absent.

You trust that the money in your bank account will be there tomorrow. You trust that the food you buy has been inspected. You trust that the contract you signed will be enforced. You trust that the person speaking to you on a video call is who they appear to be. You trust that the news article you are reading was written by a person who at least attempted to verify its claims. Every one of these trusts is so routine, so embedded in the fabric of daily life, that you do not experience them as acts of faith. They feel like facts. But they are not facts. They are agreements — agreements so widely shared that they have hardened into the invisible infrastructure on which everything else is built.

Genghis Khan understood this infrastructure better than any ruler of his age. He understood that conquest without trust is occupation, and occupation is expensive, unstable, and temporary. He built a system in which trust was not optional but structural — encoded in law, enforced consistently, and visible to everyone who participated in it. The system worked not because Mongols were unusually trustworthy people. It worked because the incentives, rules, and consequences were designed so that trusting the system was the rational choice.

And now consider what is happening to this infrastructure in your world.

In 2024, a finance worker in Hong Kong transferred twenty-five million dollars to a group of criminals after a video conference call with what appeared to be his company's chief financial officer and several other colleagues. Every face on the call was a deepfake. Every voice was synthetically generated. The worker had no way of knowing, because the technology had crossed the threshold where seeing is no longer believing.

This is not an isolated incident. It is a signal. The foundational assumption of human communication — that the person you see and hear is real — can no longer be taken for granted. AI can now generate video of people saying things they never said, in voices indistinguishable from their own, with facial expressions that match their known mannerisms. It can produce documents that appear authentic, credentials that appear verified, and identities that appear real. The tools for doing this are becoming cheaper, faster, and more accessible every month.

The implications reach far beyond financial fraud. If any video can be fabricated, then no video can be automatically trusted. If any voice can be cloned, then a phone call from your bank, your employer, or your family member is no longer self-authenticating. If any document can be forged with perfect fidelity, then the systems that rely on documentary proof — legal systems, financial systems, academic systems, immigration systems — are standing on ground that is rapidly softening.

This is not a technological inconvenience. This is an assault on the trust infrastructure of civilisation. And Genghis Khan's story tells you exactly what happens when trust infrastructure fails. It does not degrade gradually. It collapses along every seam it once held together.

But the trust crisis extends beyond deepfakes. AI is corroding trust in subtler, slower, and possibly more dangerous ways.

When a social media platform uses an AI algorithm to select which news you see, you are trusting the algorithm to surface what matters rather than what engages. That trust is, in most cases, misplaced. The algorithm is optimised for attention, not truth. The result is that millions of people are constructing their understanding of reality based on a curation system that has no commitment to accuracy and no accountability for the distortions it produces. Each person's feed confirms their existing beliefs, amplifies their existing fears, and progressively isolates them in a version of reality that fewer and fewer other people share. The shared map that Copernicus's community relied on — the common understanding that makes cooperation possible — is fragmenting. Not because people disagree. People have always disagreed. But because they no longer share enough common ground to disagree productively.

When an AI system recommends a medical treatment, produces a legal brief, or generates a financial analysis, you are trusting the system to be accurate, unbiased, and transparent about its limitations. In many cases, the system is none of these things. AI models carry the biases of their training data. They can hallucinate — producing confident, fluent, entirely fabricated information. They operate as black boxes, making decisions through processes that their own creators cannot fully explain. Trusting an AI system today is, in many ways, like trusting a doctor you have never met, in a hospital you have never visited, operating under rules you have never read. You do it because you have no practical alternative. But the trust is thin, and thin trust, as the Mongol Empire discovered, is the kind that shatters fastest.

Genghis Khan's solution was not to demand trust. It was to engineer the conditions under which trust was the rational choice. The rules were clear. The enforcement was consistent. The system applied to everyone, including the person at the top. Trust was not a feeling. It was an outcome — produced by transparency, predictability, and accountability.

This framework points directly at what the current moment requires. The trust crisis of the AI age will not be solved by appeals to honesty. It will not be solved by hoping that people behave well. It will be solved — if it is solved — by building systems in which trustworthiness is structural, not personal. Systems in which the rules are visible, the enforcement is consistent, and the consequences of betrayal are clear.

But systems are built by people. And people, before they can build trustworthy systems, must themselves be trustworthy. This is the individual dimension of Genghis Khan's lesson. In a world where reality can be fabricated, the person whose word is reliable, whose character is consistent, whose integrity has been tested and held — that person carries a kind of authority that no technology can manufacture and no deepfake can replicate. They become, in a world of synthetic everything, the one thing that is verified as real.

Trust, in the age of AI, is not just a virtue. It is the last remaining proof that you are human.

CHAPTER 7.3

CAN CIVILISATION SURVIVE WITHOUT TRUST?

Genghis Khan built the largest contiguous empire in human history on a foundation of trust. Within two generations of his death, the trust fractured, and the empire fractured with it. Not because the armies weakened. Not because the territory shrank. Because the invisible architecture that held everything together — the predictability, the fairness, the kept promises — eroded. And when trust goes, everything that was built on it goes with it, quickly and irreversibly.

The age of AI is placing the trust infrastructure of the entire world under a kind of stress it has never experienced before. Not military stress. Not economic stress. Something more fundamental: the inability to distinguish between what is real and what is fabricated. When that distinction becomes unreliable, every system that depends on it — and that is every system — is at risk.

Two directions are visible from here. And unlike the previous stories in this book, where the brighter and darker horizons felt like separate possibilities, these two futures are almost certain to coexist. The question is which one predominates.

The Brighter Horizon

In this future, the trust crisis catalyses exactly the kind of response that Genghis Khan would have recognised: the construction of new trust infrastructure, purpose-built for the conditions of the age.

Verification technologies mature. Digital signatures, blockchain-based authentication, and AI-powered detection systems create new ways to confirm that a document is genuine, a video is unaltered, and a person is who they claim to be. These systems are not perfect — the arms race between fabrication and detection is continuous — but they provide a functional floor of reliability. The Yam of the digital age is a verification layer that allows strangers to transact, communicate, and collaborate with reasonable confidence that what they are encountering is real.

But technology alone is not enough, and in this future, people recognise this. A counter-movement grows, rooted not in nostalgia but in necessity. People begin to invest in personal trust with a seriousness that previous generations reserved for professional credentials. Your reputation — not your curated online persona, but the actual, verifiable record of whether you keep your word, honour your commitments, and behave consistently — becomes your most valuable asset. Not because the world has become idealistic, but because in a sea of synthetic performance, authentic reliability commands a premium that nothing else can match.

Organisations restructure around transparency. Companies that can demonstrate, credibly and verifiably, that their AI systems are auditable, their data practices are honest, and their promises to customers are kept, outperform those that cannot. Not because transparency is a nice marketing message, but because in a low-trust environment, the entity that can be trusted attracts the resources, the talent, and the loyalty that others cannot.

In this future, trust is rebuilt. Not as the naive, default trust of previous eras — the trust that assumed a video was real because it looked real. But as a more deliberate, more robust, more consciously engineered trust. The kind that Genghis Khan built: trust as infrastructure, maintained through transparency, consistency, and accountability. Harder to build. But also harder to fake.

The Darker Horizon

In this future, the trust collapse outpaces the response.

Deepfakes become indistinguishable from reality. Detection systems, which were always running a step behind fabrication, fall permanently behind. The arms race is over, and fabrication has won. Any video, any voice, any document can be convincingly faked, and no technology can reliably distinguish the authentic from the synthetic.

The consequences are cascading and irreversible. Public discourse disintegrates. Any inconvenient evidence can be dismissed as a deepfake. Any genuine revelation can be drowned in a flood of fabricated counter-evidence. The concept of a shared reality — the common understanding that allows a society to function, to debate, to govern itself — dissolves. Not into disagreement, which is healthy, but into incompatible realities, each reinforced by its own algorithmically curated evidence, each invisible to the others.

Institutions lose legitimacy not because they fail, but because their claims can no longer be verified. A government that says the economy is growing cannot be believed, because the data could be fabricated. A company that says its product is safe cannot be trusted, because the testing records could be synthetic. A court that presents evidence cannot compel conviction, because any evidence might be artificial. The machinery of civilisation — all of it, from banking to journalism to democracy itself — runs on the assumption that evidence is real. Remove that assumption, and the machinery does not slow down. It seizes.

Society fragments into small, high-trust clusters. Families. Close friends. Local communities where people can verify each other's trustworthiness through direct, repeated, personal interaction. Global cooperation — the kind that addresses pandemics, climate change, financial crises, and technological governance — becomes effectively impossible, because cooperation at scale requires trust at scale, and trust at scale requires reliable shared information, and reliable shared information no longer exists.

This is not a science fiction scenario. Every element of it exists today, in early form. The tools are deployed. The erosion is measurable. The only question is speed: how quickly does the fabrication capability outrun the verification capability? And how much institutional trust is burned in the interval?

Genghis Khan's empire collapsed when the trust network fractured. The armies were still powerful. The territory was still vast. The infrastructure was still in place. But the invisible thing that held it all together — the belief that the rules would be followed, the promises would be kept, the system would be fair — eroded. And once it eroded past a certain point, no amount of military force, administrative brilliance, or institutional inertia could put it back together.

The parallels to the present moment are not approximate. They are precise. The trust infrastructure of the modern world is under assault from a technology that can fabricate the evidence on which trust depends. If that infrastructure fails, the consequences will not be localised or temporary. They will be civilisational.

But here is the thing about trust that Genghis Khan understood and that the darker horizon sometimes obscures: trust is not a commodity that is found or lost. It is built. Deliberately, painstakingly, through consistency, transparency, and the willingness to hold yourself accountable to the same rules you expect others to follow. It is, in the deepest sense, a choice. A choice made by individuals, repeated by communities, and scaled into institutions.

Every lesson in this book converges here. The questioning mind of Socrates, which refuses to accept a claim without testing it. The presence of Musashi, which sees clearly without the distortion of assumption. The unlearning of Copernicus, which lets go of comfortable falsehoods. The integrity of Frankl, which holds firm when everything external collapses. The storytelling of Homer, which creates the shared narratives that make trust between strangers possible. The simplicity of Lao Tzu, which cuts through noise to find the essential. Each of these is a component of trust. Each of these is a practice that, in a world where reality can be fabricated, helps you build something that cannot be faked.

The question is not whether AI will challenge the trust infrastructure of civilisation. It already is. The question is whether enough people will choose to build trust — in themselves, in their communities, in their institutions — faster than the technology can erode it.

That is the question this book has been building toward. And it is the question that only you can answer.

EPILOGUE

The Eighth Story

This book began with a dedication: a submission of my story, your story, our story — of the future. The seven stories are now told. But the book was never really about Socrates or Musashi or Copernicus or Frankl or Homer or Lao Tzu or Genghis Khan. They were the messengers. The message is for you.

The future is arriving faster than any generation has ever had to absorb. The technologies that will reshape your work, your relationships, your sense of self, and your understanding of what it means to be human are not on the horizon. They are here. And no one — no expert, no algorithm, no prophet — can tell you exactly what comes next.

What these seven stories offer is not a prediction. It is something older and more useful: a set of capacities that have held their value across every disruption, every revolution, every collapse, and every rebirth in human history. They held in Athens. They held on the steppe. They held in Auschwitz. They will hold in whatever comes next. Not because they are magic. Because they are the irreducible core of what it means to be a human being who is paying attention.

The age of AI will provide you with infinite answers, infinite content, infinite capability. It will not provide you with the question worth asking, the presence to hear the answer, the courage to let go of what is comfortable, the integrity to stand by what you believe, the story that makes someone else feel less alone, the clarity to say what matters in the fewest possible words, or the trust that turns a group of strangers into something larger than themselves.

Those are yours. They have always been yours. And the only question left is whether you will use them.

The eighth story is yours. No one else will write it.